WORD ATTACK

WORD ATTACK
A Way to Better Reading
SECOND EDITION

Clyde Roberts

*Formerly Teacher of
Remedial Reading and English,
McKinley High School, Washington, D.C.*

Illustrated by
Howard Friedman

HARCOURT BRACE JOVANOVICH
New York Chicago San Francisco Atlanta Dallas *and* London

Copyright © 1978, 1956 by Harcourt Brace Jovanovich, Inc.

All rights reserved. No part of this publication may be reproduced or transmitted in any form or by any means, electronic or mechanical, including photocopy, recording, or any information storage and retrieval system, without permission in writing from the publisher.

Printed in the United States of America

ISBN 0-15-349561-8

Contents

CHAPTER FIVE: Seeing Word Clues   61

CHAPTER SIX: Recognizing Blends   83

CHAPTER TEN: **Common Word Roots**   **111**

To the Student

Thousands of people in school and out of school are today interested in learning to read better. Colleges and universities have established reading clinics; business and military people are taking courses to improve their reading.

Reading is an essential tool in school and in business. Out of school those who read well have an advantage on any job where paper work is involved. One of the benefits of reading is growth in vocabulary. Studies of vocabularies of business people have shown that those in the higher positions usually have better vocabularies than those working under them.

It is a great advantage to anyone to have an opportunity to improve in reading while in high school.

Word Attack, which you are going to study, is calculated to make your reading more meaningful and more of a pleasure. It will show you how to conquer words that have been troublesome. You will learn how to tackle new words so that they will reveal their meaning to you. You will learn how to find in your dictionary all the interesting and helpful information about harder words. You will learn to look ahead, as a runner does before a hurdle. You will learn not to stumble at every little obstacle, back up, and come again—losing the thought.

Watch words in your reading; listen for words; make a collection of words. Words pay dividends. If you put forth effort in learning words, you will surely progress. You will improve in your school subjects. You will be better qualified for job placement. You will be a better citizen, and you will enjoy a happier intellectual life.

Clyde Roberts

WORD ATTACK

CHAPTER ONE

Some Ways of Recognizing Words and Word Groups

1. We Know a Word by the Place It Fills

Have you heard it said that people are known by the company they keep? It is the same with words. "It is getting dark. Please turn on the _____."

You can tell the word that belongs in the blank by the idea carried in the words before and after the blank.

This often happens in your daily reading. You can frequently read with no hesitation a difficult word that would puzzle you if it stood alone, just because the words before and after it suggest what it is.

Sometimes the first letter or a letter in the middle of the word clears the way.

Try this sentence: "The Sanchezes have a large orchard, and now they are shipping p____ c h____ to the city." Of course, *peaches* is not a difficult word, but you can see how letters are helpful clues.

You can usually get help from words in this way if you concentrate on meaning. You will often know a difficult word in a sentence because it is the word that fits in with the meaning of all the other words put together.

☐ Read the following sentences that have words or parts of words omitted. Can you supply the missing words?

1. Do you like your coffee without s____ and ____?

2. On the day Jane was sixteen her parents gave her a ____ party. All of the b____ and g____ in her dramatics ____b were in____, and each brought a pretty birthday ____. Ice cream and ____ were served before all left for h____.

3. After wading we dried our ____ on a large towel and walked home with our sh____ and s____ in our bags. Sharp s____ in the path caused us to walk on the green g____ beside the path.

4. Our English class gets books from the school ____ and r____ them for a few m____ in class every day.

5. A heavy snowstorm snarled t____ic, but boys and g____ dragged their s____ds to the top of the high h____ many blocks a____ and had a wonderful t____.

6. The little speckled hen flew to her n____ and sat upon her six white ____. There she seemed to be dreaming of scratching for long, fat ____ to ____ to her little brood.

7. I received a three-pound ____ of candy for a Christmas ____.

8. The monkey held out its p____ through the bars of its ____ to get the unshelled ____ the children ____ to it.

9. Labor unions sometimes s____ to obtain higher w____ and shorter h____.

10. Does the graduating class of your s____ wear c____ and g____ at the g____ exercises?

11. Do you try to study and listen to the r____ at the same ____? You should do o____ or the o____. Of course, studying and watching t____ at the same ____ is imp____.

12. Should we park the ____ here or should we put a coin in the p____ m____ around the corner?

13. Sharpen your ____ and sit in your s____ before the tardy bell ____.
14. Test time is over. Be sure your n____ is written in the upper right-hand c____ of your p____. Fold your p____ and pass it to the front of the r____.
15. Do you buy lunch in the school c____, or do you bring your ____ and eat at one of the c____ tables?
16. Senior Prom will be next F____ night. Boys may go in st____ or dr____ clothes. The town's finest or____ will furnish the ____.
17. Which color do you prefer: y____, r____, or b____ ?
18. On election day, we have a chance to v____ for the p____ we want to run our c____y.
19. The idea that each p____n has a voice is essential to a d____y.
20. Many voters do not go to the p____s but remain h____ instead.

Perhaps you found it easy to guess the word that belonged in each blank. But did members of the class sometimes disagree about what word belonged in the blank? Can you always be sure about a word by the place it fills? If not, perhaps we need other ways of knowing words. You will learn many different ways in the lessons that follow.

2. Long Words May Be Two Words Joined

Do not let length bewilder you. Sometimes a long word is just little ones joined together.

☐ Pronounce the following words. How can you account for the compounding of some of them?

1. battlefield
2. armchair
3. shipwreck
4. footstep
5. courthouse
6. lifeboat

7. silkworm
8. headstrong
9. broomstick
10. fishhook
11. nightmare
12. grapeshot
13. network
14. pushcart
15. dishcloth
16. piecework
17. kingfish
18. pancake
19. shortstop
20. pitchfork
21. shoehorn
22. seashore
23. blockhead
24. steamboat
25. basketball
26. underground
27. snapdragon
28. leapfrog
29. bookkeeper
30. playground
31. blackbird
32. headlight
33. foolscap
34. stepdaughter
35. airplane
36. grapefruit
37. starfish
38. graveyard
39. snowflake
40. hitchhike
41. fireside
42. milkweed
43. sandpaper
44. sawmill
45. pipestem
46. footlights
47. sunflower
48. toothache
49. horsepower
50. shoestring
51. oilcloth
52. landlord
53. firearms
54. porthole

3. Words Come in Thought Groups

Since our language contains many common little words of slight importance, you can take in several of these at a glance while looking ahead to a word that requires more attention. Learn to spot the convenient "stops" along the way, where you can look ahead and deal with any unfamiliar word before starting out again.

These "stops" occur between thought families, or related groups of words that must be read together because of their connection in meaning.

When you read the following groups of words you will notice that a space has been left in each line to show the "stop" between two thought "families."

□ Read the following groups of words, pausing only at the spaces between the groups.

1. on the bus   at this corner
2. along the edge   of the road
3. in my home   on this street
4. if we can ride   in your car
5. under the window   in the hall
6. for one hour   after our lunch
7. before a visit   to my friend
8. at a meeting   of the club
9. under the papers   on the chair
10. over the low fence   around the yard
11. it was in the hall   under the table
12. up the stairs   in the hallway
13. he is slow   about his work
14. within a mile   of the beach
15. some of the girls   went to the game
16. within a few months   after our visit
17. it will be easy   to find the ball
18. we want to stay   until he leaves
19. when it is raining   we ride the bus
20. she was speaking   to all of the people
21. with little children   across the street
22. when we ate lunch   at the drugstore
23. if all the boys   come to the party
24. so we can invite   all the members
25. and you will find her   on the third floor

You will easily recognize these "stops" in your own reading when there is no space to tell you.

□ From your own library book, prepare to read aloud a short paragraph, pausing for breaks between natural thought groups.

CHAPTER TWO

What the Dictionary Tells

1. Guide Words Tell Where

If you were given a fraction of a second to tell whether *u* is before or after *w*, would you have to say several letters of the alphabet to find the answer?

You might win the prize on the *u* question, but how would you fare if given a fraction of a second to tell whether you would find *mass* before or after *mast* in the dictionary? How fast are you in finding a word in the dictionary? Can you find names quickly in the telephone book? Why is it useful to be able to locate words and names quickly?

You will notice that the dictionary has timesavers that help you locate words in a hurry. These are guide words at the top of each dictionary page. Open your dictionary at any page and see if you can tell what the first and the second guide words on that page indicate.

□ Try a little game in class: Appoint a leader. The leader finds a word in the dictionary and then turns backward or forward *one* page from that word. The leader then gives the class this "new" page number; and when the class has found this page, the leader announces the selected word. The winner is the one who first tells whether to turn backward or forward to find the word announced.

2. Brackets Tell a Story

Brackets [ ] in the dictionary, found after words that are to be defined, contain extra information that is often interesting and sometimes amusing. Here you will often learn where we get our words.

Words do not just happen. They grow, change, combine, and sometimes die. Every day new words come into being. The story of a word is much like the story of a person. Mark Twain said he liked to read the dictionary to see how the characters turned out.

Read what is within the brackets next to words you look up in the dictionary. The capital letters in the brackets show through what languages a word has come down to us: Gr. — Greek; L. — Latin; AS. — Anglo-Saxon; F. — French; OF. — Old French; ME. — Middle English. This information is called the *derivation* of the word.

The large letters given above are important to advanced students of language. You will be more interested in the *other words in the brackets.* Some surprises are in store for you!

☐ Number off around the class. Each student is to select a number in the following list of words and look up the derivation of that word. While derivations are being read choose the most remarkable one. Was there one that you already knew? Take a second number on the list and see what you find this time.

1. bonfire	8. dormitory	15. demijohn
2. nicotine	9. nasturtium	16. sarcophagus
3. umbrella	10. alarm	17. tawdry
4. muscle	11. democracy	18. crucify
5. curfew	12. mausoleum	19. dinosaur
6. derrick	13. dilapidated	20. rhinoceros
7. quarantine	14. tantalize	21. jinrikisha

22. spaghetti	29. monopoly	36. carnivorous
23. ostracize	30. companion	37. mascot
24. sandwich	31. cereal	38. tulip
25. guillotine	32. pecuniary	39. canopy
26. bloomers	33. Saturday	40. maverick
27. lunatic	34. paper	
28. neighbor	35. cafeteria	

3. Parentheses Show Pronunciation

While you were consulting the dictionary, did you notice that the pronunciation appears immediately next to the word to be defined? Did you notice that the pronunciation is usually in parentheses?

When you write the pronunciation of any word, enclose it in parentheses, because this spelling is for sound only. It is always "tagged" in this way to prevent confusion.

4. Accent Marks Show Force

When you have marked all the vowels for pronunciation, you need another very important mark: the accent. Accents indicate which syllables are pronounced more forcibly. They sound a little louder than the other syllables.

Read the following sentences and see what a difference accent makes.

1. My object in coming here is to see you.
2. I do not object to your coming.

In the first sentence, which syllable of *object* gets the accent? In the second sentence, which syllable gets the accent?

If there are two accented syllables in a word, the heavier (primary) accent indicates the louder syllable. The lighter (secondary) accent indicates a syllable not quite so loud, but louder than unaccented ones. Pronounce the following words and listen to the way the syllables vary in loudness:

mis′cel·la′ne·ous   cap′il·lar′y
pre′med·i·ta′tion   fun′da·men′tal

☐ Use your dictionary to find accented syllables in the following words. See who can be first to succeed in pronouncing these hard words correctly.

1. remedial	15. errant	29. infinitesimal
2. diameter	16. polygamy	30. patina
3. gondola	17. dirigible	31. ostentatious
4. interesting	18. condolence	32. suppliant
5. infamous	19. deference	33. omnipotent
6. acclimated	20. acumen	34. exquisite
7. infidel	21. applicable	35. emissary
8. eulogy	22. apathy	36. soporific
9. longevity	23. herculean	37. sonorous
10. deficit	24. simulacrum	38. colloquy
11. comparable	25. homogeneous	39. tetrameter
12. reputable	26. desultory	40. hyperbole
13. devastate	27. increment	
14. explicit	28. superfluous	

5. Is Part of the Word Not in the Parentheses?

You will sometimes find only the last syllables, or even only the last syllable, pronounced after a word in the dictionary.

This is because pronunciation of missing syllables has already been given for another form of the word that appears above.

Count the syllables into which your word is divided; count the syllables that are pronounced after your word. Now you know how many syllables you will have to get from the pronunciation given above.

☐ Write the pronunciation of the following words.

1. wreckage
2. celebrate
3. rivalry
4. immigrate
5. abundant
6. navigation
7. repentant
8. necessity
9. elementary
10. astonishment
11. basically
12. nourishment
13. requirement
14. revolutionary

15. industrialism
16. dependency
17. diagnosis
18. intentional
19. ignoramus
20. professional
21. victimize
22. fluency
23. destitution
24. exorbitant
25. perversity
26. nebulous
27. blasphemy
28. adulatory

29. telescopic
30. physiology
31. gesticulation
32. laceration
33. opportunism
34. multiplication
35. prognostic
36. deferential
37. desiccate
38. propagation
39. reprehensible
40. insubordination

6. Can You Find Pronunciation of a Suffix?

Sometimes you will find that the final syllable of a word is not pronounced for you, either in the pronunciation given for the word or above for any other form of the word. Why?

The explanation is that these syllables that are not pronounced for you are so easy that their pronunciation can be easily remembered. They occur so many times in the dictionary that to give their pronunciation every time would result in endless repetition.

There are only a few of these syllables. You can quickly learn to write their pronunciations without hesitation. But if you do forget how one is written, all you have to do is to look up this syllable in the dictionary. It is listed separately. Remember, it will be preceded by a dash to indicate that alone it is not a word. It is called a suffix. EXAMPLE: *–ing*. What letter do we sometimes slight in saying this syllable?

☐ Write the pronunciation of the following words.

1. *–ing:*
   standing
   falling
   traveling
2. *–ly:*
   blindly
   poorly
   strangely
   tightly
3. *–ness:*
   brightness
   greatness
   strangeness

4. *–ful:*
   hopeful
   painful
   respectful
   harmful
5. *–less:*
   homeless
   strapless
   shadeless
6. *–ist:*
   vocalist
   hypnotist
   violinist

7. *–er, –or:*
   checker
   printer
   decorator
   translator
8. *–er, –est:*
   higher
   highest
   sweeter
   sweetest
   taller
   tallest

7. When Is the Final *–ed* Not a Syllable?

Pronunciation of one short addition to hundreds of words may not be given at all, either for the word or above the word. Nor is this addition pronounced the same with all words.

This mysterious addition cannot even be called a syllable, because added to some words it just merges with what goes before it.

This little puzzle is the final *–ed* you have seen thousands of times. It is not difficult to deal with, because there is a key. The key is the letters *t* and *d*.

1. If *–ed* follows the sound **t** or **d,** it is pronounced **ĕd,** a separate syllable. EXAMPLES: *planted* (plant′ĕd), *raided* (rād′ĕd).
2. If *–ed* follows any other letter sound, it is pronounced **t** or **d.** EXAMPLES: *harmed* (harmd), *ripped* (ript).

And when is it pronounced **t** and when **d?** You can very easily tell by sounding to see which "fits." Try these: *earned* (ern?); *bluffed* (bluf?). Then pronounce the words in the following list.

☐ Write the pronunciation for each of the following words.

1. counted	15. rushed	29. played
2. altered	16. tramped	30. scudded
3. depended	17. slanted	31. rooted
4. picked	18. flopped	32. destroyed
5. stuffed	19. benefited	33. prided
6. formed	20. marked	34. kicked
7. stopped	21. bossed	35. invaded
8. waited	22. pretended	36. slushed
9. locked	23. gossiped	37. cursed
10. faded	24. steamed	38. prodded
11. cashed	25. cuffed	39. gassed
12. dented	26. stressed	40. bellowed
13. compelled	27. beaded	
14. braided	28. combed	

8. Is There More Than One Correct Pronunciation?

You will occasionally find two, or even three, pronunciations of a word or of some part of a word.

These pronunciations are separated by semicolons (;) so that you can easily distinguish them.

Several dictionaries place the most preferred pronunciation (the one preferred by most educators and business people) first, and some common variations afterward. Others list multiple pronunciations according to use. The first form is the one most commonly used by most people. The front pages of your dictionary will tell you which system your book employs.

A good general rule to follow when you are in doubt about how to pronounce a certain word is to choose the first pronunciation listed.

☐ Pronounce each of the following words in two ways.

1. either (ē′thẽr; ī′thẽr)
2. neither (nē′thẽr; nī′-thẽr)
3. apparatus (ăp′a·rā′tŭs; -răt′ŭs)
4. predilection (prē′dĭ·lĕk′-shŭn; prĕd′ĭ-)
5. grenadine (grĕn′a·dēn′; grĕn′a·dēn)
6. homage (hŏm′ĭj; ŏm′-)
7. armada (är·mā′da; är-mä′da)
8. prestige (prĕs·tēzh′; prĕs′tĭj)
9. trio (trē′ō; trī′ō)
10. chassis (shăs′ĭ; -ĭs)
11. fetish (fē′tĭsh; fĕt′ĭsh)
12. vaccine (văk′sēn; -sĭn)

9. When Is a Definition Complete?

A definition ends with a semicolon (;) or a period. To stop at a comma or to stop because several words seem enough is frequently to omit the most important word of the definition.

When you write a definition, copy the entire definition. Your teacher can shorten it for you until you learn which part to select.

☐ Complete each of the following partial definitions.

1. dramatic — of or pertaining to _____.
2. preparation — act, process, or an instance of _____.

3. forward — near, at, or belonging to _____.
4. pontifical — of or having to do with _____.
5. judicial — of or pertaining or appropriate to _____.
6. speculative — of, pertaining to, or of the nature of _____.
7. hypothetical — characterized by, or of the nature of _____.
8. paternal — of or pertaining to _____.
9. treacherous — characterized by or manifesting _____.
10. emblematic — pertaining to, containing, or consisting in _____.
11. violent — moving, acting, or characterized by _____.
12. prismatic — of, pertaining to, or resembling _____.
13. volcanic — of, pertaining to, like, or characteristic of _____.
14. cadaverous — of or pertaining to, or having the qualities of _____.
15. parallelism — quality or state of being _____.
16. sentimental — of the nature of, or characterized or dominated by _____.
17. provincial — of, pertaining to, or characteristic of _____.
18. baptism — act or ceremony of _____.
19. international — common to or affecting _____.
20. contemporary — living, occurring, or existing _____.

10. Abbreviations Tell Parts of Speech in Definitions

Have you noticed the abbreviations in small italics before definitions in the dictionary?

The abbreviations are as follows: *n., v., adj., adv., pron., prep., conj., interj.*

Do you recognize them? Yes, they are the parts of speech, and you are wondering just why parts of speech should appear with all definitions. When you have had the next exercise, you will understand why.

Perhaps only the first four will concern you while you are finding definitions in the dictionary.

n.	noun: names a person, place, thing, or idea
v.	verb: expresses action or being
adj.	adjective: modifies a noun or pronoun
adv.	adverb: modifies all but a noun or pronoun

The other four are too easy for you to seek their definitions. Proof:

pron.	pronoun (EXAMPLES: *he, she, I, we,* etc.)
prep.	preposition (EXAMPLES: *to, by, in, under,* etc.)
conj.	conjunction (EXAMPLES: *and, but, or,* etc.)
interj.	interjection (EXAMPLES: *oh, whew, ouch,* etc.)

If you have a noun to define, choose the definition under *n.* If you have a verb to define, choose the definition under *v.* Adjectives and adverbs are similarly labeled.

You will find the definitions under different parts of speech for the same word usually separated by a heavy black line: —. If the part of speech you want *does not come first, look for that line;* it will shorten your looking time.

☐ In class discussion decide what part of speech each italicized word is. As the class agrees on each one, have a student with a dictionary find the definition under the part of speech you have agreed upon. In how many cases was the class correct?

1. a. Cool water *bubbles* from the little spring.
   b. Children blew *bubbles* at the birthday party.
2. a. Everybody is in a great *hurry* before Christmas.
   b. You *hurry* too much in your writing.

3. a. The *average* rainfall here is very low.
   b. Cruz made an *average* of B this semester.
   c. Most laborers *average* forty hours of work a week.
4. a. The speaker did not seem at *ease*.
   b. Hot applications will *ease* the pain.
5. a. Next Sunday will be *Mother's* birthday.
   b. The old dog *mothers* the little chicks.
   c. All our *mothers* are invited to the tea.
6. a. Where is your *home*?
   b. He made a *home* run.
7. a. Turn up the *collar* of your coat.
   b. A law requires that we *collar* and tag dogs.
8. a. The children caught several large *fish*.
   b. Crowds *fish* from the bridge on holidays.
   c. We visited the *fish* market.
9. a. Armies *sack* towns in their paths.
   b. We carried lunch in a large *sack*.
10. a. Alice Chang should not try to *rival* her sister.
    b. We had last year's champion as a *rival*.
    c. The *rival* team is from Bloomfield.
11. a. Many ships *pass* our cottage on the bay.
    b. The railroad leads through a mountain *pass*.
12. a. We drank from a cool *spring*.
    b. Annette thought the monkey would *spring*.
    c. We are enjoying the *spring* sunshine.
13. a. Julio is a very *smart* little boy.
    b. The drops caused my eyes to *smart*.
14. a. It is better to *steam* the pudding just before dinner.
    b. Brian likes to watch the *steam* from the kettle.
    c. The boat was driven by a *steam* engine.
15. a. Weeds flourish when you *neglect* your garden.
    b. *Neglect* of his homework caused his failure.
16. a. We have a large *store* of paper.
    b. Do not *store* the food in a warm place.

17. a. The thief left no *trace.*
    b. Dogs can *trace* a rabbit long distances.
18. a. *Place* your right foot forward.
    b. Our team won second *place* in the series.
19. a. All kinds of farm products were exhibited at the *fair.*
    b. The buyer offered me a *fair* price.
20. a. We worked a *quarter* of the day.
    b. The nurse had to *quarter* the apple.

11. Digits Tell How Many Definitions Under Each Part of Speech

Under each part of speech you may find several digits, or figures, when you are looking up definitions in the dictionary. These indicate various meanings from which you must select the most suitable.

If you have a noun to be defined and under *n.* you find definitions numbered 1, 2, 3, 4, read all four definitions and choose the one that "fits" the word as it is used in your sentence. You can tell which definition makes sense when you read it *into* your sentence.

You may find under a figure several letters: a, b, c. Now you select the letter that suits best after you have selected the figure that suits.

Finding definitions for words in the next exercise will help you to deal with these figures. After practice with figures, the lettered definitions will not be difficult.

☐ Choose the right definition for each italicized word in the following sentences. Each member of the class may take a group of sentences and be prepared to read the suitable dictionary definition into each sentence in place of the italicized word.

1. a. I had a cream *puff* for lunch.
   b. There was a *puff* under his right eye.
   c. The compact contains a powder *puff*.
   d. A *puff* of wind took off Dan's hat.
   e. The evening paper gives our team quite a *puff*.
2. a. The *tramp* of soldiers was heard above the music.
   b. We made the trip around the Mediterranean on a *tramp*.
   c. The *tramp* was dressed in rags and patches.
   d. We were weary after a long *tramp* in the woods.
3. a. The little *swallow* had fallen from its nest.
   b. Take one *swallow* and you will feel better.
4. a. We heard a *cardinal* singing in the park.
   b. The *cardinal* traveled here from Rome.
   c. Mary's scarf has several shades of red, but mainly *cardinal*.
5. a. He had a scar across the *bridge* of his nose.
   b. The dentist is making a *bridge* for my mouth.
   c. A new *bridge* is to be built across the river.
   d. Do you like to play *bridge?*
6. a. The sound of the bugle across the lake was *clear*.
   b. The rash soon left and my skin was *clear*.
   c. Her explanation of the error was not *clear*.
   d. The telephone line is now *clear*.
7. a. No internal *organ* was injured in the accident.
   b. My sister will play the *organ* at graduation.
   c. This magazine is our company's house *organ*.
8. a. I have math the third *period* every day.
   b. Place a *period* after a complete statement.
   c. There was great industrial development in the Victorian *Period*.
9. a. The soldier lost the *sight* of one eye.
   b. The speeding car was soon out of *sight*.
   c. The stage was a beautiful *sight* when the curtain rose.
   d. Gwen took *sight* and then fired at the target.

10. a. Do you belong to the Dramatics *Club?*
    b. The thief struck the victim with a *club.*
    c. Greg bid one diamond after I had bid one *club.*
11. a. Laws prohibit the shooting of *game* in this park.
    b. The championship *game* will be played next Friday.
12. a. Please come to the *point.*
    b. I have broken my pencil *point.*
    c. In today's game Jake made one *point* more than Brenda.
    d. What was the *point* in investing so much money?
    e. At what *point* in the West will you stop?
13. a. Not all lawyers are *rich.*
    b. Pails of milk were topped with *rich* cream.
    c. Soil of the Mississippi Delta is very *rich.*
    d. Father told us of a *rich* experience he had.
14. a. The camels rested under tall *palms.*
    b. James won the *palms* at the oratorical contest.
    c. A baby's little *palms* are soft.
15. a. Be sure you are in the *right;* then go ahead.
    b. Gail had no *right* to act in such a manner.
    c. The French president will be supported by the *right.*
16. a. Can your little brother *count* to ten?
    b. Mother can *count* on our returning by midnight.
    c. *Count* the pencils in the box, please.
    d. Personal opinion should not *count* in this question.
17. a. Traffic was routed around the *fire.*
    b. The family sat around the library *fire.*
    c. Our infantry was under *fire* for two days.
    d. The candidate was an orator of great *fire.*
18. a. Pioneers crossed the *stream* on horseback.
    b. We had never heard such a *stream* of abuse.
    c. A small *stream* of gasoline poured from the tank.

19. a. You must bring your own bat and *ball.*
    b. Earl will be dancing at the *ball.*
    c. The sun was a *ball* of fire as it sank.
20. a. This store does not *deal* in hardware.
    b. Please *deal* me a good hand.
    c. The little army will *deal* some heavy blows.
    d. The courts *deal* justly with all.

12. Words, Like People, Differ in a Group

Always be sure that you complete a definition. What does a complete definition contain?

A definition gives the group to which a thing belongs, and then gives differences between it and other things of its group. (A horse is a horse, but is it a race horse, a saddle horse, or a plow horse?)

☐ For each of the following words, you are told the group to which the thing belongs. Supply words that show the difference between the thing named and others of its group.

1. profile — a human head _____
2. bungalow — a house _____
3. buoy — a floating object _____
4. postscript — a note _____
5. compromise — a settlement of a dispute _____
6. marquee — a large field tent _____
7. penthouse — a dwelling _____
8. penitence — a feeling of pain or sorrow _____
9. labyrinth — a place full of passages _____
10. monologue — a long speech _____
11. punkah — a large portable fan _____
12. infant — a child _____

13. gaiter — a button shoe _____
14. clapboard — a narrow board _____
15. hurdle — a movable frame _____
16. ambition — an eager desire _____
17. fez — a felt or cloth hat _____
18. infantry — a body of soldiers _____
19. matinee — a musical or dramatic entertainment _____

_____

20. seaplane — an airplane _____

13. Is the Defined Word in the Definition?

Sometimes you may think it wasted labor to have looked for a definition in the dictionary.

Consider the first word in the list in the next exercise and its definition. You probably are thinking that this definition "gets me nowhere." It does seem to go in a circle, but the dictionary follows this pattern in order to prevent thousands of repetitions.

You can clear up such a definition quickly: Look above or below the definition of the word and find the definition of the "repeat" word. In looking above *legalize*, you will find *legal* defined as *lawful*.

The best way to write such definitions is as follows:

legalize — to make legal
(legal — lawful)

☐ Make necessary additions to the following definitions.

1. legalize — to make legal
2. reluctance — state of being reluctant
3. neutrality — quality of being neutral
4. ecstatic — pertaining to a state of ecstasy
5. effusion — act of effusing

6. devastation — act of devastating
7. molecular — pertaining to molecules
8. marginal — written in the margin
9. experimentation — practice by experiment
10. interjection — an interjecting
11. nourishment — that which nourishes
12. libelee — one against whom a libel has been filed
13. penetrable — capable of being penetrated
14. snobbery — snobbish conduct
15. depravity — state of being depraved
16. maturity — state or quality of being mature
17. sheathe — to put into a sheath
18. vexatious — causing vexation
19. tactician — one versed in tactics
20. optometrist — one who is skilled in and practices optometry

14. Is There a Difficult Word in the Definition?

Always be sure that you know the meaning of all words in your definition; otherwise, the word you are defining will not become a permanent and useful addition to your vocabulary.

Consider the examples below and note how the meaning of the difficult word in the definition should be shown.

1. They had brought up their children with sedulous care.
   sedulous — diligent in one's work
              (diligent — industrious)
2. She continued to make charges, despite their many renunciations.
   renunciation — act of repudiating
                  (repudiate — to refuse to accept as true)

If you read *all* definitions under the digit or the letter you have selected as best suited to your word, you may find an *easy* definition that suits as well as one with a puzzling word.

15. Illustrations Show Words in Use

The dictionary often aids you in understanding a definition by giving a sentence or phrase containing the word defined.

Watch for the little word *as*. The little word *as* introduces a sentence or phrase that illustrates. *As* and its illustration are not a definition. Do not write these as definitions.

EXAMPLES:
1. tariff — system of duties imposed by a government on goods imported; as, the *tariff* on wool.
2. breach — a breaking of waters, as over a vessel.
3. smile — to affect in a certain way with a smile; as, to *smile* away tears.
4. knickknack — a small article, as of furniture, dress, etc.
5. apparel — that which adorns; as, bright *apparel* of spring.

☐ Find two examples of the use of *as* in your dictionary.

16. Is a Word Undefined in the Dictionary?

You may some day look for a word in the dictionary and not find it at all.

One glance at the following words that might not be found in a small dictionary will probably be all you need to understand why this is so.

1. unbreakable	3. illegible	5. re-elect
2. incorrect	4. irregular	6. transplant

The dictionary avoids thousands of repetitions by not defining words that are preceded by the familiar prefix *un-*. Many of these words are listed in the dictionary, but not defined.

You probably will find definitions for all words beginning with the prefixes listed above except the prefix *un-*. But if you fail to find one beginning with any of the other five prefixes, the question is easy to handle. Look up the definition of the prefix and then look up the definition of the base word.

Prefixes are defined in the dictionary, and they can be recognized as prefixes by the dash or hyphen that follows each one to indicate that it is not a word. EXAMPLE: *ir–*

17. Synonyms Are Words Similar in Meaning

After the last definition of a word, you will sometimes find the following abbreviation in dark type: **Syn.** This is the abbreviation of *synonym*. A synonym has nearly the same meaning as the word defined.

If you read synonyms when you find them, they will make the meaning of the word you are defining much clearer. It is interesting to see, too, just how words that are much alike in meaning actually differ from each other.

The following groups of words will remind you of an exercise you have recently had (page 22). In that exercise you were given the part of the definition indicating the group to which the word belonged, and you were asked to supply the remainder of the definition, showing the difference between that word and others of its group. EXAMPLE: *bungalow* – a house.

□ Can you distinguish among all the words in any of the groups that follow? To get dictionary distinctions, look up the first word in each group, and then look under **Syn.**

1. trade
craft
business
profession
2. implement
tool
utensil
instrument
3. less
smaller
fcwcr
4. destiny
fate
doom
5. assume
affect
pretend
simulate
feign
6. face
countenance
visage
physiognomy

7. dispute
quarrel
wrangle
squabble
bicker
8. solitary
alone
lonely
lonesome
lone
desolate
9. melancholy
sadness
dejection
gloom
10. dilate
expand
distend
inflate
11. pity
sympathy
compassion
condolence

12. move
actuate
impel
prompt
incite
instigate
13. fluctuate
oscillate
vibrate
vacillate
waver
14. defend
protect
guard
preserve
15. effect
execute
perform
discharge
accomplish
achieve

18. Antonyms Are Words Opposite in Meaning

Following the last definition of a word and sometimes following **Syn.**, you may find another abbreviation: **Ant.** This is the abbreviation of *antonym.* An antonym has a meaning opposite to the meaning of the word defined.

☐ Examine the following groups of words to understand antonyms. Notice that all the antonyms for a word are, among themselves, synonyms. For dictionary aid look up the numbered word and find **Ant.**

1. *transparent*
   opaque
   murky
   clouded
   obscured
2. *solve*
   complicate
   involve
3. *cordial*
   cool
   distant
   unfriendly
   hostile
4. *busy*
   disengaged
   unemployed
   inactive
   idle
5. *mercy*
   cruelty
   harshness
6. *extemporaneous*
   prepared
   planned
   designed
   calculated
7. *servile*
   noble
   haughty
8. *less*
   more
   greater
9. *strength*
   feebleness
   frailty
10. *melancholy*
    joy
    gaiety
    merriment
    happiness
    gladness
11. *strict*
    liberal
    lenient
    unrestrained
12. *assume*
    reject
    decline
    doff
    deny

19. Homonyms Are Words Similar in Sound

Words that have the same pronunciation but usually differ in spelling and always differ in meaning are *homonyms*. EXAMPLES: *bear, bare.*

Words of each pair in the following list either are homonyms or are so much alike in pronunciation and spelling that they are often confused.

Be sure you are familiar with this list. Is there another "pair" of words that confuses you when you are writing?

☐ Which of the following pairs are homonyms?

1. there   their
2. lose   loose
3. woman   women
4. fare   fair
5. weather   whether
6. coarse   course

7. aloud allowed	14. stationery stationary
8. whole hole	15. which witch
9. quiet quite	16. dyeing dying
10. presents presence	17. capital capitol
11. piece peace	18. waist waste
12. here hear	19. principal principle
13. raise rays	20. plain plane

20. Labels Tell by Whom Words Are Used

Any different-looking type that you see among definitions of a word in the dictionary (any print that differs from the rest) is a guide meant to aid you.

This type that differs may be italics or capital letters. It is used for special labels like the following:

Slang   Indicates the word is not standard usage.

Colloq.   *Colloquial* — indicates the word is used in familiar conversation.

Obs.   *Obsolete* — indicates the word is no longer in use.

Law   Definition following is one used in law.

Math.   Definition following is one used in mathematics.

See   This is followed by a word you are to find in the dictionary. Sometimes this other word has a picture to illustrate it, indicated by *Illust.*

Find several other labels in your dictionary.

21. Pronunciation Guides Tell Letter Sounds

No mention has been made of the guides to pronunciation found at the foot of each right-hand page of most dictionaries. If you forget the sound of some letter or some letter combination, consult this pronunciation guide and your memory will be refreshed. Small dictionaries sometimes have a pronunciation guide inside the front cover only, not on each right-hand page.

Some dictionaries use systems of marking somewhat different from those you have learned. But the sounds of the letters are the same in all dictionaries. If you know these sounds and have learned one marking system, you can easily interpret another.

22. Gazetteer and Biographical Dictionary Tell Important Facts

Most dictionaries contain a Gazetteer and a Biographical Dictionary in the back of the book. If you wish to find any geographical information, consult the Gazetteer. If you wish to find information about any prominent person, consult the Biographical Dictionary.

If any character or geographical item is imaginary, it will not be found in the Biographical Dictionary or the Gazetteer, but in regular alphabetical order in the main part of the dictionary. EXAMPLES: Pandora — an imaginary character; Lilliput — an imaginary land.

Some dictionaries also contain in the back alphabetical arrangements under the following headings:

1. Abbreviations Used in Writing and Printing
   EXAMPLE: R.S.V.P.
2. Common Given Names
   EXAMPLES: Lionel — young lion
   Sarah — a princess
3. Foreign Words and Phrases
   EXAMPLE: *à la carte*
4. Tables of Weights and Measures
   EXAMPLE: 1 kilogram = 2.2 pounds

Dictionaries can be of great assistance if you know how to use them.

☐ Find in the dictionary information on the following names:

1. John Paul Jones
2. Helen of Troy
3. Clara Barton
4. Tecumseh
5. Ebenezer Scrooge
6. Joan of Arc

☐ Consult your dictionary for information about the following places:

1. Amsterdam
2. Utopia
3. Richmond
4. Elysium

☐ Find for what each of the following abbreviations is a shortened form:

1. M.D.
2. C.I.A.
3. C.O.D.
4. Fahr.
5. F.O.B.

☐ What "meaning" has each of the following names?

1. Don Juan
2. Cassandra
3. Pollyanna
4. John Hancock
5. Hoyle

☐ Consult your dictionary for a translation of the following foreign phrases. (The more familiar foreign phrases will be found in the larger section of the dictionary, as these are becoming, or have become, a part of our language.)

1. bona fide
2. coup d'état
3. in loco parentis
4. à la carte

Test on the Dictionary

1. If *fair* and *fall* are guide words on page 297 in a dictionary, you know that *family* is not defined on that page. You know you must turn forward, not backward, to find *family*.

In Column A below, certain guide words are listed with their page numbers. In Column B are words to locate. Choose a page number for each word in Column B, selecting the one on which you would expect to find that word defined.

Column A	Column B
1. condemn — conduction (page 210)	conclusion — page 209 or 211?
2. chastisement — checkmate (page 172)	cheerful — page 171 or 173?
3. don — dorsal (page 300)	dormant — page 299, 300, or 301?
4. realizer — rebound (page 828)	realism — page 827, 828, or 829?
5. strangely — stream (page 984)	strength — page 983, 984, or 985?

2. Copy the second column and supply the missing symbols that show the derivation of each word.

6. pen   from *penna,* feather
7. conform   kŏn fôrm′
8. gelatin   from *gelare,* to freeze
9. terrace   from *terra,* earth
10. general   jĕn′ēr·ăl
11. obscure   ŏb·skūr′
12. rectory   rĕk′tō·rĭ
13. champion   from *campus,* battlefield
14. ditto   dĭt′ō
15. hippopotamus   from *hippos,* horse + *potamos,* river

3. Copy the following words as they are shown divided into syllables; mark the accented syllable.

16. mon u ment
17. sub scrip tion
18. ther mom e ter
19. di plo ma
20. li brar y

4. Label each of the following pairs as synonyms, antonyms, or homonyms.

21. black — white
22. hard — difficult
23. pity — sympathy
24. wear — ware
25. eternal — temporary

5. In what section of the dictionary would you find information on each of the following?

26. Florence Nightingale
27. Niagara
28. Helen Keller
29. Labrador
30. Jupiter and Neptune
31. Queen Victoria
32. Hades
33. Land of Promise
34. Louisiana
35. Santa Claus

6. How does your dictionary "tag" the italicized words to show the difference between the words in each pair of sentences?

36. The parade will *circle* the big city park.
37. Angie drew a large *circle* on the blackboard.
38. The monkey held out its *hand* for the candy.
39. Please *hand* me my book from the table.
40. We had a *test* in math yesterday.
41. The gym exercises *test* one's endurance.
42. There were *double* doors at each entrance.
43. Delivering newspapers will *double* my income.
44. Western farmers *plant* large fields of wheat.
45. Tobacco is a large-leafed *plant*.

7. What should be added to each of the following definitions to make the meaning clear?

46. bell — a hollow metallic vessel _____
47. sword — a weapon _____
48. helicopter — a form of aircraft _____
49. banjo — a stringed musical instrument _____
50. pyramid — a massive structure _____

CHAPTER THREE

How Vowels Are Sounded

Sometimes words contain letters that are silent, like *a* in *coat,* but most letters in words are sounded. Five very important letters of the twenty-six in our alphabet have more than one sound each. These are the vowels: *a, e, i, o, u* (and *y* when it sounds like *i*).

Since every word in our language contains at least one vowel, our language would be quite humdrum if each of the five vowels always were sounded the same.

In the dictionary, vowels have tags, called diacritical marks, that indicate their different sounds. By means of these diacritical marks we are able to tell just how to pronounce any new and unfamiliar word.

The following exercises will give you practice in the vowel sounds.

Long *a* and Short *a*

Long *a:* ā āpe   **Short *a:* ă ăpple**

☐ Copy the following words and mark each *a* long or short. You will have to pronounce each word to know which mark to add.

1. shape	10. tame	19. wagon	28. tack
2. cash	11. tassel	20. navy	29. safe
3. paper	12. sand	21. plant	30. lash
4. rain	13. chapter	22. saddle	31. wafer
5. faint	14. cake	23. brass	32. lamb
6. plank	15. native	24. came	33. jacket
7. table	16. paint	25. made	34. radish
8. marry	17. magnet	26. gate	35. flat
9. gravy	18. cave	27. hand	36. trace

Long *e* and Short *e*

Long *e*: ē ēagle   **Short *e*:** ĕ ĕgg

☐ Copy the following words and mark each *e* long or short. You will have to pronounce each word.

1. credit	10. seat	19. shell	28. team
2. vest	11. echo	20. yellow	29. shield
3. cream	12. dent	21. pencil	30. melon
4. feast	13. seldom	22. demon	31. second
5. pedal	14. lesson	23. leaf	32. deal
6. equal	15. penny	24. tell	33. scream
7. cedar	16. heath	25. field	34. Venus
8. shed	17. plead	26. help	35. felt
9. flesh	18. legal	27. ferry	36. peony

Long *i* and Short *i*

Long *i*: ī īce

Short *i*: ĭ ĭgloo

☐ Copy the following words and mark each *i* long or short. You will have to pronounce each word to know which mark to add.

1. lion	11. knit	21. white	31. right
2. wild	12. dizzy	22. slide	32. high
3. pinch	13. mice	23. shiver	33. widen
4. silk	14. fire	24. fish	34. quilt
5. clip	15. night	25. wick	35. differ
6. child	16. ring	26. fright	36. ride
7. ridge	17. silly	27. print	37. give
8. file	18. rival	28. life	38. pike
9. pick	19. ditch	29. lift	39. skip
10. frill	20. minor	30. mink	40. quill

Long *o* and Short *o*

Long *o*: ō ōak

Short *o*: ŏ ŏx

☐ Copy the following words and mark each *o* long or short. You will have to pronounce each word to know which mark to add.

1. note	11. hobby	21. gosling	31. politics
2. float	12. scold	22. motive	32. robin
3. pocket	13. bold	23. rock	33. stop
4. tonsil	14. notice	24. novel	34. moment
5. stone	15. pond	25. blow	35. solid
6. clover	16. blot	26. shop	36. gold
7. soft	17. cold	27. dome	37. toddle
8. frog	18. colic	28. post	38. proper
9. dollar	19. goat	29. soap	39. coach
10. roast	20. donkey	30. foam	40. stove

Long *u* and Short *u*

Long *u*: ū ūkulele   **Short *u*: ŭ ŭmbrella**

□ Copy the following words and mark each *u* long or short. You will have to pronounce each word to know which mark to add.

1. music	11. number	21. tune	31. funeral
2. lunch	12. bucket	22. unity	32. rubber
3. rustle	13. durable	23. button	33. bubble
4. bugle	14. brush	24. must	34. gulf
5. hunt	15. rumor	25. truck	35. duty
6. plus	16. public	26. fume	36. crucial
7. custom	17. husband	27. pure	37. pulp
8. Tuesday	18. duke	28. blunt	38. fuel
9. mule	19. duck	29. tulip	39. rudder
10. lunatic	20. pump	30. luggage	40. mush

Other Vowel Sounds

Italian or "two-
dot" *a:* ä   färm

Tilde *e:*
ē   pẽrcolator

Tilde *i:*
ĩ   bĩrd

Circumflex *o:*
ô   ôrgan

Circumflex *u:*
û   tûrtle

Notice that these vowels sound as if the *r* has some influence.

But the letter *r* does not always affect them. Sometimes one of these sounds occurs when *r is absent.* EXAMPLE: *fäther.* Sometimes the vowel is not pronounced as above when *r is present.* EXAMPLE: *bĕrry.*

Notice that these sounds of *e, i,* and *u* are similar. You may find in pronunciations in your dictionary a respelling for some of them. EXAMPLES: *fern* (fûrn), *bird* (bûrd).

☐ All five vowels are included in this lesson because you will encounter these spellings in your reading. Copy these words and mark all vowels that have sounds similar to those listed above.

1. arch	germ	circle	horse	burn
2. dart	verse	flirt	cord	turf
3. harp	derby	whirl	horn	purple
4. mark	verb	firm	order	burden
5. scarf	mercy	third	lord	turban
6. card	stern	girl	corn	hurt
7. barley	certain	chirp	torch	spur
8. palm	swerve	skirt	orphan	curl
9. margin	servant	birch	north	turn
10. bargain	vermin	dirk	fork	curtain
11. arsenic	berth	stir	scorch	murmur
12. guitar	learn	birth	orchard	gurgle
13. parsnip	hermit	twirl	border	survey
14. charm	perform	squirm	torpedo	furnish
15. tardy	earth	mirth	ornament	nursery

Test on Vowels

Copy the following words and mark each vowel. Notice that the final *e* is silent. Mark silent vowels with an X through them.

If you look up the pronunciation of one of these words in your dictionary, you may find for a vowel a long mark with a tiny bar in the center. EXAMPLES: *obey* (ȯ·bā′), *unite* (ŭ·nīt′). This bar appears because the long vowel is not in the accented syllable.

1. supervise	11. corner	21. thirteen
2. pedestal	12. horizon	22. cardinal
3. holiness	13. darling	23. closet
4. vitality	14. cracker	24. interest
5. thirsty	15. survive	25. argument
6. carnival	16. upper	26. rescue
7. nativity	17. opponent	27. torment
8. benefit	18. subscribe	28. trigger
9. republican	19. microscope	29. scarlet
10. ivory	20. hypodermic	30. terminate

31. important	38. continual	45. tornado
32. ordnance	39. dormitory	46. obscure
33. peanut	40. fortunate	47. ignorant
34. curbstone	41. bursting	48. lobster
35. spider	42. larkspur	49. ostrich
36. absolute	43. hippopotamus	50. logical
37. circumstance	44. barbecue	

Half Italian *a*

Half Italian or "one-dot" *a:*
ȧ   sofȧ

Your dictionary probably shows you an *a* with one dot, called the half Italian *a*. This *a* has half as many dots as ä (**ärm**), and is not quite so broad when spoken.

☐ Pronounce the following words to get the sound of ȧ. What words can you add to this list?

1. soda	15. arithmetic	29. notable
2. delta	16. gondola	30. America
3. Ella	17. panda	31. miserable
4. tuba	18. rumba	32. hexagon
5. among	19. phobia	33. legacy
6. alert	20. petunia	34. sympathy
7. Stella	21. buffalo	35. obstacle
8. amidst	22. tentacle	36. pyramid
9. abode	23. ornament	37. temperature
10. diploma	24. chickadee	38. about
11. ago	25. escadrille	39. lucrative
12. begonia	26. viaduct	40. senator
13. orchestra	27. cockatoo	
14. adore	28. liability	

Circumflex *a*

Circumflex *a:*
â châir

Your dictionary shows an *a* marked **â.** Pronounce this almost as you do short *a.*

☐ Note the sound of circumflex *a* in the following words.

1. âir	4. fâre	7. hâir	9. lâir
2. câre	5. beâr	8. pâir	10. prâyer
3. wâre	6. stâir		

Long Double *o* (o͞o) and Short Double *o* (o͝o)

Long *oo:* o͞o bo͞ot   Short *oo:* o͝o bo͝ok

☐ Pronounce the following words to get these sounds.

1. droop	8. sloop	1. took	8. brook
2. cool	9. food	2. wool	9. stood
3. tooth	10. goose	3. look	10. moor
4. moon	11. soon	4. cook	11. crook
5. stool	12. broom	5. soot	12. wood
6. fool	13. loop	6. poor	13. good
7. boom	14. proof	7. nook	14. book

☐ What words can you add to each list?

The Slur

Slur: tu picture

Slur: du educate

Only one other diacritical mark will you need when pronouncing vowels from their diacritical marks in the dictionary: the slur. The slur occurs with both tu and du. It indicates a single sound for the combination of these letters.

It takes a keen ear to notice this odd pronunciation of tu and du, but you have heard it daily. Pronounce the following words and get the slur sound.

1. future
2. creature
3. feature
4. lecture
5. nature
6. fracture
7. century

8. texture
9. overture
10. pasture
11. fortune
12. torture
13. temperature
14. architecture

15. forfeiture
16. scripture
17. spiritual
18. saturate
19. perpetuate
20. venture
21. miniature

1. verdure
2. pendulum
3. procedure
4. arduous

5. fraudulent
6. adulation
7. credulous
8. gradual

9. modulate
10. nodular
11. glandular
12. sedulous

☐ What words can you add to this list?

y as a Vowel

Sometimes *y* is a vowel, sounding like *i*, long or short.

☐ Copy the following words and beside each write the letter *i* and mark it long (ī) or short (ĭ).

1. my	6. myth	11. mystery	16. cyclone
2. very	7. badly	12. typhoon	17. tyranny
3. eye	8. likely	13. cypress	18. supply
4. type	9. tyrant	14. pyramid	19. gymnasium
5. spry	10. cylinder	15. gypsy	20. symbol

CHAPTER FOUR

How Consonants
Are Sounded

As you encounter more unfamiliar words in your reading, you will need skill in sounding the consonants and their combinations.

Can you sound **l** by itself? The combination **bl?** Do you know the sound of **qu?** If you do, you have a good start.

The following exercises will give you practice in sounding the consonants and will train your ear in catching their sounds when you hear them.

The first group in each exercise generally contains words with the special letter-sound at the beginning of the word; the second group generally contains words with the sound at the end of the word; and the third group generally contains words with the sound inside the word.

Be sure to remember each *key word.* These come to your aid when you hesitate in pronouncing the sounds and have no list before you.

Consonant *b*

b   **boy**

☐ Pronounce these words, listening for the sound of **b**.

1. bad	21. rib	41. rabbit
2. bug	22. tab	42. fabric
3. bid	23. sob	43. rebel
4. bell	24. fib	44. tablet
5. brass	25. Bob	45. hobble
6. band	26. cab	46. lobster
7. boot	27. tub	47. rubber
8. blush	28. bib	48. dabble
9. bird	29. web	49. object
10. brown	30. rob	50. absurd
11. bolt	31. snob	51. nibble
12. but	32. grab	52. above
13. bin	33. stab	53. public
14. bag	34. crib	54. liberal
15. black	35. slab	55. clabber
16. bank	36. throb	56. table
17. beat	37. crab	57. double
18. berry	38. rub	58. gable
19. bring	39. nab	59. lobby
20. board	40. knob	60. babble

Consonant *d*

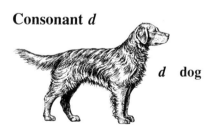

d   dog

☐ Pronounce the following words, listening for the sound of **d**.

1. do	3. dull	5. dish
2. die	4. deep	6. date

7. dent	25. gold	43. meadow
8. dug	26. sad	44. toddle
9. dome	27. pod	45. saddle
10. duke	28. lead	46. fodder
11. deck	29. hard	47. cadet
12. dear	30. add	48. hundred
13. dim	31. grand	49. adore
14. dare	32. yard	50. index
15. deal	33. read	51. haddock
16. dull	34. said	52. needle
17. drake	35. bend	53. lady
18. drum	36. need	54. adorn
19. drug	37. lard	55. madame
20. doom	38. skid	56. admit
	39. period	57. maiden
	40. orchid	58. dedicate
21. mad		59. reduce
22. nod		60. federal
23. road	41. puddle	
24. end	42. ladle	

Consonant *f*

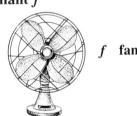

f **fan**

☐ Pronounce these words to hear the sound of f. Can you tell when *f* doubles at the end? (What kind of vowel precedes each double *f* in words of one syllable?)

1. foot	5. fox	9. fence
2. fell	6. fun	10. feel
3. food	7. fat	11. feet
4. fog	8. fin	12. felt

13. flash	29. reef	45. offer
14. flow	30. ruff	46. ruffle
15. from	31. shelf	47. offend
16. freeze	32. scarf	48. refuse
17. field	33. staff	49. baffle
18. flit	34. thief	50. rifle
19. fish	35. dwarf	51. traffic
20. from	36. gruff	52. reform
	37. stuff	53. office
21. puff	38. loaf	54. safety
22. chief	39. half	55. thrift
23. leaf	40. buff	56. shuffle
24. stiff		57. terrific
25. gulf	41. taffy	58. purify
26. self	42. muffin	59. notify
27. skiff	43. trifle	60. coffee
28. golf	44. suffer	

Consonant *g*

g   **goat**

☐ In pronouncing the following words listen for the sound of g.

1. game	8. good	15. grave
2. goose	9. glide	16. gulf
3. gun	10. gash	17. globe
4. golf	11. grain	18. gain
5. gate	12. glass	19. gospel
6. grape	13. greed	20. gave
7. glad	14. glow	

21. fig
22. hug
23. beg
24. pig
25. bug
26. dug
27. log
28. bag
29. fog
30. mug
31. big
32. rug
33. snag
34. twig

35. slug
36. clog
37. bog
38. nag
39. pug
40. drug

41. organ
42. igloo
43. tiger
44. legal
45. buggy
46. English
47. August

48. magazine
49. haggle
50. ignite
51. program
52. magnolia
53. negative
54. figure
55. ignorant
56. ignore
57. trigger
58. frugal
59. elegant
60. dragon

Consonant *h*

h   hat

☐ Pronounce these words, listening for the sound of **h**.

1. hen
2. hut
3. had
4. hip
5. hall
6. hog
7. head
8. horse
9. hoop
10. happy

11. home
12. heel
13. high
14. hood
15. half
16. hero
17. hair
18. house
19. hedge
20. help

21. Ohio	31. dehydrate
22. Oklahoma	32. abhor
23. behoove	33. inhibit
24. inhabit	34. mahogany
25. inherit	35. behave
26. prohibit	36. inhuman
27. exhume	37. Mohawk
28. mishap	38. rehearse
29. adhere	39. Yahoo
30. inhale	40. Mohammedan

Consonant *j*

j   jug

☐ Pronounce the following words and listen for the sound of **j.**

1. job	14. Jack
2. jet	15. jerk
3. jay	16. juice
4. jaw	17. jewel
5. jig	18. junk
6. jolt	19. James
7. jump	20. judge
8. join	
9. jam	21. major
10. jelly	22. object
11. joke	23. majestic
12. John	24. project
13. jury	25. rejoice

26. injustice
27. adjourn
28. enjoy
29. reject
30. adjust
31. conjure
32. unjust
33. misjudge

34. prejudice
35. rejuvenate
36. adjective
37. injury
38. adjacent
39. projectile
40. inject

Consonant *k*

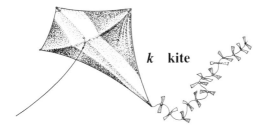

k kite

☐ Pronounce the following words to learn the sound of **k**. Notice the letter *c* in words numbered from 21 through 40. Every *c* is silent. What does *c* separate? Explain the absence of *c* in five of these words.

1. kill
2. keg
3. king
4. keen
5. kit
6. kid
7. keel
8. kick
9. key
10. kiss
11. kind
12. keep
13. kink

14. kilt
15. Kelly
16. kettle
17. kindle
18. kerchief
19. kitchen
20. kimono

21. back
22. mock
23. pork
24. tuck
25. lock

26. pick
27. black
28. peck
29. duck
30. neck
31. risk
32. link
33. luck
34. deck
35. pack
36. sick
37. smoke
38. knock

39. plank	46. nickel	54. cackle
40. trick	47. pickle	55. poker
	48. tickle	56. trickle
41. turkey	49. market	57. cricket
42. monkey	50. broken	58. sparkle
43. musket	51. okra	59. rocket
44. napkin	52. pocket	60. bracket
45. basket	53. token	

Consonant *l*

l **leaf**

☐ Pronounce the following words and listen for the sound of **l**. What does double *l* not follow?

1. last	17. lamb	32. hull
2. loaf	18. long	33. seal
3. loop	19. line	34. peel
4. letter	20. lemon	35. nail
5. light		36. real
6. late	21. tell	37. squeal
7. leap	22. call	38. snail
8. lake	23. hill	39. spell
9. lung	24. sell	40. shall
10. lamp	25. tall	
11. lord	26. mill	41. jelly
12. leak	27. bell	42. yellow
13. look	28. pull	43. pillow
14. land	29. kill	44. mellow
15. life	30. pill	45. village
16. lace	31. Bill	46. melon

47. salad	51. holy	55. truly
48. gallon	52. lily	56. wallet
49. silver	53. follow	57. Sally
50. dollar	54. pulley	58. lilac

Consonant *m*

m man

☐ Pronounce the following words, listening for the sound of **m**.

1. mad	20. boom	39. humor
2. milk	21. hum	40. imagine
3. much	22. skim	41. lamp
4. meat	23. gum	42. stamp
5. mouse	24. room	43. slumber
6. march	25. stem	44. lumber
7. mile	26. beam	45. thimble
8. map	27. bum	46. summer
9. medal	28. seem	47. temple
10. melon	29. elm	48. sermon
11. music	30. film	49. lemon
12. mouth	31. term	50. human
13. mail	32. ream	51. number
14. mutton	33. trim	52. hammer
15. major	34. worm	53. glimmer
16. motto	35. scum	54. simple
17. maple	36. gloom	55. timid
18. muddy	37. steam	56. nimble
19. merry	38. roam	57. tumble

Consonant *n*

n newspaper

☐ Pronounce the following words, listening for the sound of **n**.

1. nap	21. tin	41. hunt
2. not	22. fun	42. sand
3. neck	23. den	43. find
4. navy	24. ran	44. pantry
5. north	25. gun	45. linen
6. night	26. swan	46. paint
7. note	27. train	47. funeral
8. neat	28. grain	48. tender
9. nurse	29. loan	49. vanish
10. name	30. learn	50. kindle
11. nest	31. skin	51. manner
12. nice	32. person	52. tenant
13. number	33. satin	53. honey
14. noose	34. broken	54. lantern
15. nerve	35. golden	55. partner
16. noise	36. token	56. hundred
17. noble	37. green	57. mineral
18. needle	38. pardon	58. Nancy
19. nation	39. bean	59. money
20. nickel	40. pelican	60. plunder

Silent *k* precedes *n* at the beginning of many words:

1. knew	3. knob	5. knight
2. knit	4. knave	6. knot

7. knock	11. knoll	15. knead
8. know	12. knuckle	16. knapsack
9. knowledge	13. knee	17. knickknack
10. knell	14. knife	18. Knickerbocker

Notice that each of the first eight in the list would be a different word with a different meaning without the silent *k*. Write these eight words without the *k* and see if you know their meanings.

Remember these silent *k* words when you are spelling.

Consonant *p*

p   pan

☐ Pronounce the following words for the **p** sound.

1. pill	16. paint	30. romp
2. puff	17. peach	31. lump
3. plan	18. punch	32. grasp
4. pass	19. penny	33. wrap
5. poke	20. pencil	34. skip
6. pine		35. hump
7. perch	21. cup	36. gulp
8. plow	22. lip	37. wasp
9. post	23. map	38. soap
10. pick	24. tip	39. trap
11. paw	25. nap	40. stamp
12. pray	26. sip	
13. pink	27. top	41. supper
14. prize	28. reap	42. rapid
15. peer	29. slip	43. vapor

44. sample	50. slipper	56. tipsy
45. lapel	51. tepee	57. sloppy
46. paper	52. simple	58. torpedo
47. napkin	53. temper	59. stampede
48. maple	54. purple	60. opponent
49. open	55. hamper	

Consonant *r*

r   rat

☐ Pronounce these words, listening for the sound of **r**.

1. red	18. rapid	34. star
2. rule	19. rattle	35. spear
3. rice	20. radish	36. spire
4. rose		37. locker
5. rank	21. fur	38. ulcer
6. rush	22. bar	39. armor
7. roast	23. sir	40. pastor
8. rug	24. nor	
9. ride	25. tar	41. sorry
10. ranch	26. leer	42. parlor
11. ring	27. near	43. furrow
12. root	28. scar	44. turkey
13. race	29. pair	45. garment
14. rich	30. jar	46. person
15. raw	31. brier	47. market
16. rock	32. hair	48. sermon
17. river	33. poor	49. narrow

54   WORD ATTACK

50. sherbet
51. garland
52. German
53. party

54. harbor
55. marry
56. hurdle
57. Jerry

58. marine
59. orchard
60. charity

Consonant *s*

s snake

☐ Pronounce the following words and note the sound of s.

1. sack
2. side
3. seed
4. soda
5. sun
6. sky
7. sift
8. scar
9. send
10. snow
11. spade
12. smell
13. soap
14. slice
15. spring
16. screw
17. snail
18. slap
19. supper
20. spider

21. boss
22. miss
23. toss
24. kiss
25. fuss
26. tress
27. bless
28. guess
29. yes
30. Swiss
31. press
32. glass
33. pass
34. muss
35. hiss
36. moss
37. this
38. recess
39. confess
40. unless

41. sister
42. gossip
43. listen
44. blast
45. possess
46. lesson
47. rascal
48. basin
49. aspic
50. hospital
51. possible
52. person
53. glisten
54. massive
55. tassel
56. arsenic
57. testify
58. respect
59. estate
60. custard

Consonant *s* Sounding like *z*

Sometimes *s* has the sound of z.

☐ Pronounce the following words to get this sound.

1. is	14. boys	26. raisin
2. has	15. girls	27. easy
3. lose	16. rooms	28. palsy
4. rise	17. schools	29. misery
5. fuse	18. lunches	30. music
6. was	19. riches	31. cosmetics
7. choose	20. tools	32. hesitate
8. use		33. wisdom
9. wise	21. closet	34. muslin
10. rouse	22. busy	35. husband
11. raise	23. rosary	36. residence
12. please	24. cousin	37. Thursday
13. abuse	25. nasal	

☐ What words can you add with the suffix *-ism?*

Consonant *t*

t   toad

☐ Pronounce the words listed to get the sound of **t.**

1. toy	6. tune	11. tool
2. tank	7. timber	12. trick
3. tooth	8. tax	13. test
4. tub	9. tea	14. tusk
5. tree	10. tire	15. table

16. talk	31. soft	46. matter
17. twig	32. skirt	47. sitting
18. type	33. trot	48. fetter
19. train	34. tight	49. distance
20. tulip	35. sheet	50. lantern
	36. left	51. system
21. fist	37. melt	52. mental
22. just	38. slant	53. printer
23. best	39. smart	54. spatter
24. lost	40. guilt	55. meditate
25. rust		56. shutter
26. nest	41. Latin	57. mitten
27. last	42. butter	58. pattern
28. dust	43. little	59. letter
29. rest	44. nutmeg	60. estate
30. sweet	45. dentist	

Consonant *v*

v   vase

☐ Pronounce the following words, listening for the sound of v.

1. vote	8. verb	15. vinegar
2. vest	9. valve	16. victim
3. very	10. veto	17. village
4. voice	11. verse	18. vanish
5. view	12. velvet	19. volcano
6. vine	13. violin	20. valentine
7. visit	14. vanity	

21. gave	35. thrive	48. savage
22. save	36. alive	49. ivory
23. love	37. strive	50. govern
24. move	38. leave	51. seven
25. nerve	39. curve	52. novel
26. hive	40. wave	53. convoy
27. glove		54. travel
28. rove	41. ivy	55. invest
29. serve	42. oval	56. convert
30. grave	43. level	57. navigate
31. shove	44. never	58. revenge
32. above	45. cover	59. service
33. olive	46. fever	60. peevish
34. grieve	47. gravel	

Consonant *w*

w   watch

☐ Pronounce the following words for the sound of the letter *w*. (Final *w* is sometimes silent after *o*. Example: *yellow*.)

1. wife	11. wink	21. sweet
2. wolf	12. well	22. twitch
3. weed	13. wire	23. swear
4. wall	14. word	24. forward
5. wise	15. wash	25. sweat
6. wait	16. wool	26. beware
7. web	17. work	27. dwarf
8. wick	18. wing	28. twill
9. wave	19. west	29. swallow
10. weak	20. world	30. twist

31. dwindle	35. twice	39. swan
32. twine	36. reward	40. twinkle
33. inward	37. swamp	
34. dwelling	38. twirl	

Consonant *y*

y   yoke

☐ Pronounce the following words to get the sound of the consonant **y**.

1. yet	5. yarn	9. yacht	13. youth
2. yes	6. your	10. year	14. yonder
3. you	7. young	11. York	15. yellow
4. yell	8. yeast	12. yield	16. Yankee

Letter *y* as a Vowel and as a Consonant

You have learned that *y* is sometimes a vowel and sometimes a consonant.

☐ Number your paper from 1 to 16. After the number of each of the following words, write *y* if *y* is a consonant and write long *i* or short *i* if *y* is a vowel.

Can you draw any conclusion as to when *y* is a consonant?

1. Yahoo	5. mystery	9. funny	13. typhoid
2. style	6. yucca	10. hurry	14. Yugoslavia
3. yak	7. Yule	11. gypsy	15. yearn
4. system	8. dynamo	12. July	16. yarrow

Consonant *z*

z zebra

☐ Pronounce the following words and listen for the sound of **z**.

1. zoo	19. prize	37. Brazil
2. zero	20. freeze	38. buzzard
3. zone	21. jazz	39. sizzle
4. zest	22. buzz	40. frozen
5. zinc	23. haze	41. gizzard
6. zipper	24. seize	42. lazy
7. Zulu	25. fuzz	43. blizzard
8. zeal	26. quiz	44. crazy
9. zither	27. blaze	45. horizon
10. zodiac	28. maize	46. dazzle
11. Zion	29. breeze	47. brazen
12. zenith	30. squeeze	48. frizzle
13. zephyr	31. trapeze	49. gazette
14. zinnia	32. sneeze	50. lozenge
15. zircon	33. razz	51. razor
	34. snooze	52. puzzle
16. size	35. raze	53. gazelle
17. graze		54. vulcanize
18. friz	36. lizard	55. mezzanine

CHAPTER FIVE

Seeing Word Clues

Now that you have had lessons in learning to pronounce words by using the dictionary, you are going to consider some ways of finding how to pronounce words without the dictionary.

It will be a great help in reading to be able to tackle a new word and determine its pronunciation or meaning by analysis.

A clue will help not only in pronouncing little words, but also in pronouncing longer words. Frequently a clue helps with a syllable, and the syllable is a clue to the entire word.

Final-*e* Clue

When a word ends in *e*, the *e* is usually silent and the vowel before it is usually long.

☐ Pronounce each pair of the following words.

1.	fin	fine	7. twin	twine
2.	hat	hate	8. dim	dime
3.	cut	cute	9. pal	pale
4.	not	note	10. rip	ripe
5.	bit	bite	11. van	vane
6.	tub	tube	12. Sam	same

13. man	mane		27. win	wine
14. kit	kite		28. plum	plume
15. hop	hope		29. prim	prime
16. pan	pane		30. slim	slime
17. strip	stripe		31. rot	rote
18. tap	tape		32. quit	quite
19. shin	shine		33. sham	shame
20. rid	ride		34. fat	fate
21. mat	mate		35. fad	fade
22. pin	pine		36. Tim	time
23. sit	site			
24. Jan	Jane			
25. shad	shade			
26. hid	hide			

Double-Vowel Clue

When two vowels occur together in a word, frequently the second vowel is silent and the first vowel is long.

☐ Copy the following words and mark all vowels. Mark silent vowels with an X through them.

1. road	11. foam	21. beat	31. sail
2. steam	12. please	22. coat	32. seat
3. coach	13. jail	23. pail	33. ream
4. reap	14. braid	24. neat	34. heap
5. meal	15. loaf	25. soak	35. peach
6. rail	16. preach	26. stream	36. soap
7. beam	17. gait	27. nail	37. seal
8. heat	18. lean	28. load	38. toad
9. clean	19. goat	29. mean	39. meat
10. leaf	20. bail	30. plead	40. tail

Sometimes two vowels occurring together in a word are in separate syllables, and then both vowels are sounded.

☐ Pronounce the following words.

1. duel	3. cruel	5. real	7. gruel
2. trial	4. fuel	6. dial	8. poet

What other words can you think of that contain two vowels occurring together, each sounded?

Digraphs *au* and *aw* Clue

The combinations *au* and *aw* nearly always have the sound of circumflex *o* (ôrgan). These combinations are called *digraphs* (*di* = two; *graph* = writing): two writings (letters) with one sound for the two.

☐ Pronounce the following words and remember these combinations of letters when you find them in reading.

1. auburn	13. auditor	24. saucer
2. August	14. automatic	25. jaunt
3. audience	15. Austria	26. faucet
4. aurora	16. Austin	27. gauze
5. Australia	17. autumn	28. cauldron
6. auction	18. austere	29. slaughter
7. automobile	19. augment	30. sausage
8. authority	20. auger	31. vault
9. authentic		32. laundry
10. autopsy	21. Paul	33. saunter
11. author	22. caution	34. haul
12. auditorium	23. launch	35. fault

1. awl	6. draw	11. law
2. awe	7. straw	12. craw
3. awful	8. claw	13. raw
4. awkward	9. flaw	14. saw
5. awning	10. paw	15. squaw

16. thaw	22. hawthorn	29. brawn
	23. gawky	30. prawn
17. crawl	24. scrawny	31. spawn
18. hawk	25. dawdle	32. pawn
19. bawl	26. tawdry	33. squawk
20. scrawl	27. crawfish	34. tawny
21. sprawl	28. brawl	35. lawn

ei-ie Clue

1. Combination *ei* following *c* generally fits the Double-Vowel Clue.
2. Combination *ei* without this *c* is generally sounded ā. It may be followed by silent letters.
3. Combination *ie* reverses *ei* and generally "reverses" the Double-Vowel Clue (*first* vowel is silent and *second* vowel is long).

☐ Pronounce the following words that illustrate the three parts of the *ei–ie* Clue. (Another way to remember *ei-ie* pronunciation: *ie* and *ei* (after *c*) have the sound of ē; *ei* (without *c*) has the sound of ā.)

1. ceiling	3. receipt	5. deceit	7. conceit
2. receive	4. deceive	6. conceive	8. perceive

1. eight	4. neigh	7. skein
2. weight	5. feign	8. rein
3. sleigh	6. vein	9. reign

1. field	6. liege	11. thief	16. shield
2. chief	7. belief	12. relief	17. lief
3. wield	8. lien	13. piedmont	18. siege
4. piece	9. niece	14. achieve	19. shriek
5. grief	10. priest	15. brief	20. believe

☐ Learn these so that you can spell them from dictation.

eu-ew Clue

The combinations *eu* and *ew* are generally pronounced ū or o͞o. Sometimes both pronunciations will be given in your dictionary for the same word. EXAMPLE: *jewel* (jo͞o′ĕl; jū′ĕl).

Each of the words in the first and second columns has the sound of ū; each of those in the third column has the sound of o͞o.

□ Pronounce these words.

1. feud	1. dew	1. flew
2. neuron	2. sewage	2. screw
3. Aleutian	3. mew	3. blew
4. neutral	4. few	4. grew
5. Teuton	5. Lewis	5. crewel
6. deuce	6. knew	6. clew
7. pneumonia	7. pew	7. shrew
8. neuritis	8. lewd	8. brew
9. leucite	9. gewgaw	9. threw
10. pneumatic	10. pewter	10. slew
11. neuralgia	11. hew	11. shrewd
12. leukemia	12. new	12. crew
13. Europe	13. mildew	13. drew
14. eulogy	14. spew	14. strew
15. euphony	15. askew	15. Newton
16. eugenics	16. steward	16. Matthew
17. eucalyptus	17. sinew	17. brewery
18. eureka	18. curlew	18. chew
19. euchre	19. ewer	19. view
20. Euclid	20. ewe	20. yew
21. euphemism	21. Jewish	21. newt
22. euphoria	22. newspaper	22. Stewart
23. Eugene	23. skewer	23. trews
24. euglena	24. Dewey	24. threws

Diphthong *oi (oy)* Clue

oi coins

oy oyster

The dictionary defines a diphthong as a speech sound changing from one vowel to another in the same syllable. Say the sounds ô (ôrgan) and ĭ (ĭgloo) rapidly in succession, and they will seem to merge. The **oy** diphthong sounds the same. Do you associate the well-known sound with the spelling without hesitation? As this sound is always the same, there is no diacritical marking.

☐ Pronounce the following words.

1. oil	15. loin	29. boil
2. Boyd	16. boy	30. goiter
3. voice	17. poison	31. McCoy
4. broil	18. noise	32. toil
5. poise	19. alloy	33. soy
6. coil	20. toy	34. Troy
7. point	21. voile	35. doily
8. join	22. employ	36. embroider
9. Joy	23. loiter	37. boisterous
10. hoist	24. moist	38. thyroid
11. void	25. roister	39. destroy
12. annoy	26. spoil	40. poinsettia
13. cloister	27. loyalty	
14. soil	28. tabloid	

Diphthongs *ou* and *ow* Clue

ou house   *ow* owl

The sound of these diphthongs is one you also know, but do you always associate the sound with the letters?

Note that these two diphthongs sound the same, and your dictionary may show **ou** as the pronunciation of both spellings: *how* (hou). The sound represented by **ou** in dictionary pronunciation is always the same, so no diacritical marking is needed.

☐ Pronounce the following words.

1. stout	10. trout	19. ounce	28. crowd
2. pound	11. about	20. proud	29. down
3. loud	12. scout	21. cow	30. drown
4. count	13. voucher	22. allow	31. brown
5. mouse	14. gout	23. town	32. vowel
6. found	15. slouch	24. crown	33. flower
7. snout	16. cloud	25. now	34. tower
8. doubt	17. louse	26. clown	35. coward
9. bound	18. mouth	27. brow	36. dowry

Test on Vowel Word Clues

☐ Write the number for each of the following words, and after each number write the *letter* from the following list that indicates the clue for the word.

a. Final-*e* Clue	d. *cei* Clue	g. *eu-ew* Clue
b. Double-Vowel Clue	e. *ei* Clue	h. *oi(oy)* Clue
c. *au-aw* Clue	f. *ie* Clue	i. *ou-ow* Clue

1. snake	16. carouse	31. shade	46. wheat
2. fraud	17. shape	32. growler	47. smoke
3. deceit	18. naughty	33. deploy	48. receipt
4. frail	19. poise	34. streak	49. powder
5. steward	20. steal	35. creek	50. sheep
6. trawler	21. brake	36. mouse	51. yawl
7. flake	22. convoy	37. feudal	52. spiel
8. croak	23. fear	38. flea	53. sewer
9. fiend	24. pouch	39. shriek	54. enshroud
10. newel	25. papaw	40. whale	55. while
11. foil	26. Beulah	41. macaw	56. ceiled
12. stroke	27. Pete	42. white	57. embroil
13. endow	28. freight	43. announce	58. thews
14. brain	29. subsoil	44. twain	59. applaud
15. beige	30. trousers	45. pleurisy	60. bead

Double-Consonant Clue

Double consonants in a word usually indicate a short vowel sound before the double consonant.

Many words double the final consonant before a suffix beginning with a vowel. Both these and other double-consonant words usually have a short vowel sound before the double. EXAMPLES:

1. dim: dimming, dimmer, dimmest
   snap: snapping, snapper, snapped
   drop: dropping, dropper, dropped

2. buggy, tattle, minnow,
   bubble, silly, twiddle, suffer

Final-*e* words usually drop the *e* before suffixes beginning with a vowel. EXAMPLES:

advise, advisable; write, writing; please, pleasure

☐ Write the number of each of the following words. Then, pronouncing the words one by one, copy each word, and mark the first vowel of each word long or short.

1. wining	16. scrapped	31. tuned	46. citing
2. wined	17. rider	32. bottom	47. finest
3. winning	18. ridden	33. twining	48. batter
4. dinning	19. riding	34. canning	49. bater
5. dined	20. ridding	35. chasing	50. batted
6. dining	21. using	36. shipping	51. batting
7. writing	22. jammed	37. placing	52. bating
8. written	23. tunnel	38. gaping	53. pinned
9. scraping	24. stripping	39. gapping	54. pining
10. scraper	25. striping	40. hummed	55. pinner
11. scraped	26. stripped	41. canned	56. pinning
12. flatten	27. striped	42. caned	57. hoped
13. redden	28. stripper	43. canner	58. hoping
14. scrapping	29. tuning	44. caning	59. hopping
15. scrapper	30. tuner	45. snobbish	60. hopped

Consonant *c* Followed by *e* or Followed by *i(y)* Clue

Consonant *c* is sounded in several ways. When *c* is followed by *e* or *i(y)*, it has the sound of **s** (**snake**). When *c* is combined with *h*, the two have a sound all their own. (The **ch** sound will be given later in word clues.) When *c* is followed by any other letter it has the sound of **k** (**kite**).

☐ Pronounce the following words and notice the sound *c* has.

1. cent	11. cider	21. placid	31. lancet
2. cell	12. cypress	22. piece	32. decide
3. cement	13. citrus	23. silence	33. deceit
4. celery	14. cymbal	24. spice	34. bicycle
5. cellar	15. circle	25. vicinity	35. incite
6. century	16. cylinder	26. specific	36. twice
7. center	17. cinder	27. biceps	37. Pacific
8. celebrate	18. cigar	28. fleece	38. incidence
9. cereal	19. citizen	29. lucid	39. recital
10. censor	20. ceremony	30. tacit	40. receive

1. cab	11. college	21. because	31. describe
2. collar	12. cross	22. scarlet	32. lecture
3. curtain	13. club	23. second	33. narcotic
4. clover	14. coast	24. discuss	34. picture
5. crow	15. castle	25. economy	35. recover
6. cold	16. custom	26. delicate	36. scurry
7. clasp	17. coffee	27. concrete	37. indicate
8. candy	18. cuff	28. tobacco	38. victory
9. crumb	19. creek	29. political	39. acre
10. calf	20. curve	30. locate	40. dedicate

☐ Write the number of each of the following words and after each number write *s* or *k* for the sound of *c* in the word. If there is more than one *c* in a word, write *s* or *k* for each one.

1. canvas	11. celebrity	21. bacteria	31. alcohol
2. clown	12. cinnamon	22. evacuate	32. license
3. city	13. cringe	23. notice	33. masticate
4. ceiling	14. crumble	24. pacify	34. Cupid
5. curb	15. crocodile	25. income	35. facility
6. cease	16. cigarette	26. vacancy	36. arctic
7. cream	17. clean	27. licorice	37. bicuspid
8. coat	18. citadel	28. vacuum	38. acre
9. canoe	19. receptacle	29. client	39. peculiar
10. cricket	20. cemetery	30. optical	40. erect

Sounding Both *c*'s

When double *c* occurs in a word and the second *c* has the sound of **s**, don't fail to pronounce the first *c*. This first *c* has the sound of **k**.

☐ Pronounce the following words and listen for the **k** sound for the first *c*.

1. accent	5. acceptance	9. accession
2. accelerate	6. access	10. eccentric
3. accident	7. accessible	11. occident
4. accept	8. accessory	12. occipital

Consonant *g* Followed by *e* or Followed by *i*(*y*) Clue

Consonant *g* has regularly a sound of its own, which was given with the consonant sounds (page 46). But when *g* is followed by *e* or *i*(*y*), it often has the sound of **j** (**jug**).

☐ Pronounce the following words and note how *g* sounds like **j**. Why is silent *e* necessary in the words numbered 21-40?

1. giant	11. generous	21. judge
2. general	12. Gibraltar	22. siege
3. gelatin	13. Georgia	23. lounge
4. giraffe	14. generate	24. cabbage
5. ginger	15. geometry	25. orange
6. germ	16. German	26. fringe
7. gentle	17. gist	27. range
8. gypsy	18. genius	28. pledge
9. giblet	19. gentry	29. large
10. gesture	20. gymnasium	30. rage

31. badge	41. eligible	51. magic
32. trudge	42. pigeon	52. vegetable
33. purge	43. tragedy	53. fidget
34. strange	44. frigid	54. legitimate
35. plunge	45. manger	55. fledgling
36. stage	46. algebra	56. legislature
37. verge	47. fugitive	57. margin
38. nudge	48. tragic	58. prodigy
39. foliage	49. longitude	59. lethargy
40. dirge	50. agent	60. Argentina

☐ Write the number of each of the following words and beside each number write a *g* or a *j* to indicate the sound of each *g* in the word.

1. gender	21. engage
2. goose	22. regular
3. gas	23. vagrant
4. goblet	24. pageant
5. generation	25. wagon
6. grand	26. geography
7. glass	27. magnet
8. genial	28. wager
9. gem	29. fragile
10. grass	30. program
11. gutter	31. wedge
12. genuine	32. August
13. grit	33. manage
14. good	34. codger
15. geranium	35. dragon
16. gold	36. segment
17. glad	37. original
18. grime	38. congeal
19. game	39. vagabond
20. gallon	40. region

The *h* Family

You have seen that *c* and *g* are frequently influenced by *e* and *i*(*y*).

Consonant *h* is a very "influential character." Sounds of the following *h*-combinations will be given you in the following exercises so that you can see how influential *h* really is.

ch	gh	sh	wh
chr	ph	th	

☐ Consonant *h* is even sounded as if it were present with *s* or with *z* in a few words when it is actually not present at all. (In such words *s* has the sound of **z**.) Note the key word for the **zh** sound.

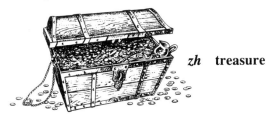

zh   treasure

1. pleasure	5. exposure	9. azure
2. vision	6. composure	10. brazier
3. leisure	7. decision	11. glazier
4. collision	8. measure	12. seizure

Digraph *ch* Clue

ch   church

When *c* and *h* are together the sound is usually like that heard in **church.** You will hear the one sound of the two letters **ch** when pronouncing the following words.

1. chain	21. snatch	41. satchel
2. chimney	22. reach	42. butcher
3. chuckle	23. catch	43. luncheon
4. chin	24. ditch	44. mischief
5. cheese	25. peach	45. teacher
6. chalk	26. flinch	46. watchful
7. chicken	27. hatch	47. wretched
8. cheer	28. ranch	48. poacher
9. charm	29. trench	49. bleaching
10. cherry	30. stretch	50. archery
11. chunk	31. match	51. preacher
12. choke	32. pinch	52. Fletcher
13. churn	33. search	53. pitcher
14. chose	34. witch	54. slouchy
15. chest	35. Scotch	55. latchet
16. Charles	36. couch	56. merchant
17. chew	37. pitch	57. sketchbook
18. cheek	38. sketch	58. achieve
19. chill	39. thatch	59. discharge
20. charge	40. stitch	60. exchange

☐ Notice the letter *t* preceding *ch* in many words of the second and third columns. Every such *t* is silent. What does this *t* separate? Explain the absence of this *t* in twenty of the words in these two columns. (This will aid you in spelling.)

chr Clue

When *ch* is followed by *r,* usually the *h* is silent, so the *c* sounds like **k,** the sound of *c* and *r* being brought together.

☐ Pronounce the following words.

1. Christmas
2. chrome
3. chromatic
4. Chrysler
5. chronic
6. chrysanthemum
7. chromite
8. chronological
9. chrysalis
10. chrism
11. chromium
12. Christian
13. Christine
14. christen
15. chromosome

gh Clue

In some words the combination *gh* has the sound of **f.**
In other words *gh* is silent. Notice in the following words
that when *gh* is silent the letters are usually followed
by *t*.

☐ Pronounce these words.

1. laugh
2. cough
3. rough
4. tough
5. trough
6. enough

1. right
2. ought
3. weight
4. taught
5. night
6. might
7. bought
8. plight
9. height
10. fraught

11. Dwight
12. light
13. sight
14. freight
15. sought
16. fought
17. nought
18. tight
19. fight
20. straight

☐ How are *bough* and *dough* exceptions to the general
rule? Can you think of other exceptions?

ph Clue

The combination *ph* generally has the sound of **f (fan).**

□ Pronounce the following words.

1. phone
2. phrase
3. phlox
4. physics
5. Philip
6. pharmacy
7. philosophy
8. pheasant
9. phonics
10. photostat
11. Phyllis
12. phantom
13. phase
14. phobia
15. pharynx
16. phial
17. philharmonic
18. photographer
19. phrenology
20. philander

21. telegraph
22. nymph
23. triumph
24. phonograph
25. sylph
26. Ralph
27. Joseph
28. paragraph

29. nephew
30. siphon
31. alphabet
32. gopher
33. prophecy
34. orphan
35. pamphlet
36. phosphorus
37. typhoon
38. Ophelia
39. morphine

40. sophomore
41. naphtha
42. diphtheria
43. hydrophobia
44. phosphorescent
45. typhoid
46. dolphin
47. asphalt
48. amphibian
49. delphinium
50. geography

Digraph *sh* Clue

sh   **sheep**

When *s* and *h* are together, the sound is usually like that heard in **sheep.** You will hear the one sound of the two letters **sh** when you pronounce the words listed on the next page.

1. sheet	21. hush	41. bishop
2. shop	22. dash	42. worship
3. sharp	23. rash	43. astonishment
4. shift	24. rush	44. freshet
5. shirt	25. bush	45. bushel
6. shave	26. fish	46. cashew
7. shin	27. gash	47. cashier
8. shall	28. wish	48. threshold
9. Sharon	29. hash	49. usher
10. shun	30. dish	50. Washington
11. shrub	31. mesh	51. cashmere
12. shield	32. blush	52. Bolshevik
13. shiver	33. mush	53. ashamed
14. shore	34. brush	54. bashful
15. shrink	35. wash	55. marshmallow
16. shelter	36. push	56. fleshy
17. should	37. trash	57. dashboard
18. shudder	38. swish	58. mushroom
19. shampoo	39. goulash	59. seashore
20. shoulder	40. distinguish	60. beshrew

Digraph *th* Clue

th teeth

~~*th*~~ teethe

When *t* and *h* are together, the two generally combine into one of two sounds, as heard in **teeth** and **teethe**. Your dictionary probably distinguishes between the two sounds of *th* by marking the latter thus: **~~th~~**. This is the one diacritical mark used only for consonants.

You can detect the difference between the two *th* sounds by pronouncing the following words. (Notice that the *th* sound in **teeth** is voiceless and in **teethe** is voiced.)

☐ List the numbers of the following words that have the voiced sound. You may have to consult your dictionary sometimes.

1. thick	23. bath	41. mother
2. the	24. bathe	42. father
3. thistle	25. wreath	43. brother
4. this	26. wreathe	44. author
5. thief	27. mouth	45. leather
6. their	28. scathe	46. thither
7. three	29. cloth	47. rather
8. these	30. clothe	48. Catholic
9. thaw	31. breath	49. heathen
10. that	32. breathe	50. southern
11. thorn	33. death	51. Bethlehem
12. those	34. north	52. slither
13. thumb	35. south	53. hither
14. them	36. Ruth	54. weather
15. thought	37. both	55. athlete
16. though	38. heath	56. ether
17. thread	39. Smith	57. whither
18. throat	40. truth	58. whether
19. thresh		59. method
20. thunder		60. neither
21. thin		
22. then		

wh Clue

When *w* and *h* are together, the *h* usually moves over in front of *w* in sound: **wh** sounds **hw.**

When you pronounce the following words you will notice an **h** (**hat**) sound before the **w** (**watch**) sound.

1. whiff	6. wheeze	11. wheat	16. whisker
2. when	7. wheel	12. whip	17. whittle
3. whale	8. what	13. whether	18. whet
4. while	9. whim	14. wharf	19. white
5. where	10. whine	15. whisper	20. whirl

Digraph *ng* Clue

ng   wing

The digraph **ng** represents the sound heard in *sing, ring,* which is different from the sound of **n** plus the sound of **g**.

Sometimes *n* alone has this **ng** sound, usually when followed by *g* or *k: anger* (ăng′ger); *ink* (ĭngk).

Words in the first group below contain words with the **ng** sound when *g* is present. Do not sound the *g* separately.

Words in the second group contain words with *n* sounding **ng** because *g* follows the letter *n.*

Words in the third group contain words with *n* sounding **ng** because *k* (or *c* sounding like *k*) follows the letter *n.*

1. bring	5. bang	9. young
2. sling	6. song	10. length
3. thing	7. long	11. strength
4. fling	8. strong	12. The suffix "-ing"

1. anger (ăng'gēr)
2. congress (kŏng'grĕs)
3. anguish (ăng'gwĭsh)
4. tangle (tăng'g'l)
5. wrangle (răng'g'l)
6. bangle (băng'g'l)
7. Bangkok (băng'kŏk)
8. finger (fĭng'gēr)
9. shingle (shĭng'g'l)
10. angle (ăng'g'l)
11. language (lăng'gwĭj)
12. tingle (tĭng'g'l)

1. drink (drĭngk)
2. think (thĭngk)
3. bunk (bŭngk)
4. uncle (ŭng'k'l)
5. trunk (trŭngk)
6. mink (mĭngk)
7. blank (blăngk)
8. honk (hŏngk)
9. junk (jŭngk)
10. kink (kĭngk)
11. junction (jŭngk'shŭn)
12. tincture (tĭngk'tûr)
13. sanctify (săngk'tĭ·fī)
14. function (fŭngk'shŭn)

qu Clue

The letter q has no sound of its own. It is always followed by the letter u, and the combination qu has the sound of kw in most words; but in some words it has the sound of k only, as in French.

The words numbered 1-39 have the kw sound. Words numbered 1-12 at the top of page 81 have the k sound.

In pronouncing the following words you will learn to distinguish the two groups.

1. quack
2. quail
3. quit
4. quiet
5. quart
6. queen
7. quick
8. quote
9. quill
10. quiver
11. quaint
12. quarrel
13. quality
14. question
15. quake
16. quantity
17. quarry
18. quadruped
19. quadrille
20. quintet
21. equal
22. square
23. squeal
24. squeeze
25. squall
26. squadron
27. sequence
28. soliloquy
29. Iroquois*
30. equestrian

* Iroquois: final letter is silent, as in French.

31. liquid	1. croquet*	8. catafalque
32. squash	2. croquette	9. grotesque
33. sequel	3. etiquette	10. burlesque
34. squirrel	4. briquette	11. picturesque
35. squelch	5. coquette	12. statuesque
36. equip		
37. frequent	Endings of *que:*	
38. equator	6. antique	
39. sequin	7. oblique	

x Clue

Consonant *x* has no sound of its own. It has the sound of **ks** in most words.

Probably you have not noticed that in words beginning with *ex* the *x* sometimes has the sound of **gs**: *examine* (ĕg·zăm′ĭn), *exact* (ĕg·zăkt′).

Some technical terms used in the sciences begin with the letter *x*, and here the sound of *x* is that of **z**. The only word you will encounter in this group at this time probably is *xylophone* (zī′lȯ·fōn).

X is one of the three letters that have no sounds of their own: *c*, *q*, and *x*.

☐ Pronounce the following words.

1. box	11. jinx	21. next	31. exercise
2. tax	12. lox	22. oxygen	32. mixture
3. fox	13. ax	23. maxim	33. excite
4. wax	14. ox	24. flexible	34. Baxter
5. six	15. lax	25. excavate	35. fixture
6. flax	16. crux	26. textbook	36. vexation
7. coax	17. fix	27. excuse	37. saxophone
8. phlox	18. smilax	28. Maxwell	38. Mexico
9. mix	19. relax	29. tuxedo	39. buxom
10. vex	20. equinox	30. maximum	40. lexicon

* *Croquet:* final *et* is pronounced ā, as in French.

CHAPTER SIX

Recognizing Blends

Consonants are usually separated in words or syllables by vowels: *bake, dominate*.

Consonants *l, r, s,* and *t* when not separated from *some* consonants may blend with these consonants: flake, farm, snow, tent. At the end of words, *m* and *n* may make a few blends: ro**mp,** sa**nd.**

When blends occur at the beginning of words or syllables they are called *initial blends,* and when they occur at the end they are called *final blends.*

In the division of words into syllables, blends are not separated.

Combinations of the "*h* family" are not blends. These combinations (such as **sh**ine, **ph**one, **th**is) make *one* sound each and do not blend *two* sounds, except **wh.** They may blend with some consonants: bi**rch,** **shr**imp, ea**rth.**

In the following exercise you are going to make samples of the initial blends. This will be like working an easy crossword puzzle.

To make samples of final blends would take much longer, because these cannot be found alphabetically arranged in dictionaries.

Sometimes a final blend may be an inversion (a turning around) of an initial blend: **fl**ake, se**lf**; **dr**ay, boa**rd**; **tr**ay, hu**rt.**

To recognize initial or final blends watch for *l, r, s,* and *t,* and also for *m* and *n* at the end of words or syllables.

Many plural forms are examples of final blends:

1. books	4. chins	7. yards
2. shops	5. jackets	8. roofs
3. jobs	6. flags	9. paths

Initial Blends

☐ Write the following heading for your paper: Initial Blends. Bear in mind that you are to make four columns of words on your paper.

1. Number one through seven for your first column. After each number leave space for one letter and write the letter *l* for each of the seven numbers.

    In the spaces before the letter *l* try one by one the letters in the following list until you make a blend that begins a word. Write each word as you find it. Use each item in the following list only once in the first column.
    List: b, c, d, f, g, h, j, k, l, m, n, p, qu, r, s, t, v, w, x, z, ch, ph, sh, th (*qu* is itself a blend of **k** and **w**, but it can also be preceded by a letter in the list to form another initial blend.)

2. Number one through eleven for your second column. After each number leave space for one letter and write the letter *r* for each of the eleven numbers.

    In the spaces before the letter *r* try one by one the letters in the above list until you make a blend that begins a word. Write each word as you find it. Use each item in the list only once in this second column.

3. Number one through thirteen for your third column.* Write the letter *s* immediately after each number in your third column.

---

* *Note:* In the third column you will find three blends that you have made which will give three more if you add *r* as the third letter in the blend: str____; and one more if you add *l* as the third letter in the blend: spl____.

Immediately after the letter *s* try each of the letters in the list on page 84 until you make a blend that begins a word. Write each word as you find it. Use each item in the list only once in this third column.

4. Number one through two for your fourth column. Write the letter *t* immediately after each number in your fourth column.

Immediately after the letter *t* try each of the letters in the list on page 84 until you make a blend that begins a word. Write each word as you find it. Use each item in the list only once.

When you have completed your paper you will have a sample of the initial blends, except one: *dw.* make two words for this blend below the fourth column.

Test on Blends

☐ Write the number for each of the following words and then write the blend found in the word of each number.

1. complex	16. unscrew	31. refrigerate
2. ensnare	17. declare	32. serfdom
3. pressure	18. immigrate	33. engulf
4. sharpen	19. intrude	34. mostly
5. enthrone	20. sprocket	35. emblem
6. vagrancy	21. between	36. caprice
7. conglomerate	22. refresh	37. bondage
8. jolted	23. decry	38. enshrine
9. encrust	24. trial	39. celebrate
10. pumped	25. forswear	40. obscurity
11. inspire	26. alarmed	41. besmear
12. shrinkage	27. entwine	42. afloat
13. stealth	28. distribute	43. despondent
14. firmer	29. besmirch	44. enslave
15. deprive	30. comply	45. bestir

46. emblaze
47. destroy
48. reclaim
49. discern
50. nutriment
51. explicit
52. monster
53. risky
54. conclude
55. bestride

56. reflect
57. supreme
58. defraud
59. diploma
60. bestow
61. selfish
62. adopted
63. dissolve
64. nucleus
65. lurched

66. mirthful
67. cobra
68. girlish
69. cypress
70. nymph
71. contrive
72. table
73. dawdle
74. twice
75. abduct

CHAPTER SEVEN

Dividing Words into Syllables

You have found that sometimes when words looked difficult, they were only two short, easy words put together. And you found that at other times when words looked difficult, little words could be found in them, and from these little words you could build to the whole word.

Learning to divide words into syllables is most important in learning to read and to spell better. Syllabication, or the dividing of words into syllables, enables you to take bit by bit words that are not as easy as just two joined together or a little one with added letters. You divide and conquer.

A few principles govern the dividing of words into syllables. The following exercises will give you practice in applying these principles or rules. Practice in syllabication will enable you to tackle any long word with confidence.

Principle One in Syllabication

When there are *two* consonants between two vowels, syllable division is generally between the two consonants.

☐ 1. Copy the following words and underscore each vowel. (This is an important step. EXAMPLE: w<u>i</u>nd<u>o</u>w.)

2. Write the word beside the underscored one, dividing it into syllables. EXAMPLE: win dow.

Now you are in a position to see how division into syllables aids in pronunciation in a second way: When a vowel is last in a word or syllable, it is usually *long*. *Vowels in other positions are usually short* unless the *r* following makes them ä, ē, ī, ô, û. Final *a* is sometimes pronounced ȧ. EXAMPLE: sō fȧ.

3. Mark all the vowels in your divided-word column. EXAMPLE: wĭn dōw (*w* is silent, so *o* sound is last).

Do not forget that some final letters are silent. Mark these letters with an X.

1. rabbit	11. paddock	21. goblet	31. parka
2. permit	12. carpet	22. fellow	32. yellow
3. burden	13. cellar	23. signal	33. master
4. basket	14. hello	24. garment	34. hammer
5. motto	15. circus	25. victim	35. magnet
6. ladder	16. murmur	26. garter	36. pardon
7. pencil	17. lantern	27. border	37. corner
8. aspic	18. sister	28. problem	38. bandit
9. rumba	19. dinner	29. fabric	39. tender
10. silver	20. garden	30. rascal	40. barber

Principle Two in Syllabication

When there is *one* consonant between two vowels, syllable division is usually *before* the consonant.

☐ **1.** Copy the following words and underscore each vowel. This is important. EXAMPLE: below.

2. Write the word beside the underscored one, dividing it into syllables. EXAMPLE: be low.

3. Mark all vowels. EXAMPLE: bē lōw.

1. solo	3. pupil	5. veto	7. tulip
2. lilac	4. spiral	6. labor	8. spider

9. vacant	17. taper	25. sober	33. wafer
10. tiger	18. basin	26. halo	34. vital
11. favor	19. polo	27. final	35. totem
12. silent	20. meter	28. cedar	36. major
13. raven	21. total	29. open	37. Homer
14. molar	22. razor	30. saber	38. fatal
15. divan	23. paper	31. rival	39. solar
16. Juno	24. zero	32. pilot	40. item

Principle Three in Syllabication

Words that end in *le* preceded by a consonant are divided before this preceding consonant. EXAMPLE: tur tle.

The exception to this rule is the "pickle" group, words that end in *ckle*. EXAMPLES: *tickle, tackle, shackle.* Here *c* is silent and the *k* goes with the first syllable. EXAMPLE: pick le.

☐ **1.** Copy the following words, dividing them into syllables.

    2. Mark the vowels.

1. mumble	11. simple	21. twinkle	31. sickle
2. buckle	12. knuckle	22. tangle	32. stumble
3. jingle	13. sample	23. hurdle	33. purple
4. gable	14. fickle	24. gurgle	34. ventricle
5. marble	15. thistle	25. barnacle	35. fumble
6. trample	16. humble	26. hustle	36. wrangle
7. table	17. monocle	27. whistle	37. bungle
8. uncle	18. single	28. dwindle	38. circle
9. ladle	19. noble	29. bustle	39. Myrtle
10. bumble	20. spindle	30. crumble	40. trickle

Principle Four in Syllabication

When *-ed* is added to a word that ends in a **t** or **d** sound, the *-ed* is a separate syllable. EXAMPLES: test ed, bond ed.

When -ed is added to a word that does not end in a **t** or **d** sound, -ed is not a separate syllable. EXAMPLE: walked, tramped.

☐ 1. Copy the following words, dividing them into syllables.
  2. Mark the vowels.

Note: grade — graded (final *e* dropped): grād ĕd
  bud — budded (final letter doubled): bŭd dĕd

1. bolted	11. hunted	21. lashed	31. tasted
2. waited	12. folded	22. fished	32. carved
3. liked	13. planted	23. scolded	33. dated
4. parted	14. weeded	24. thudded	34. spaded
5. gushed	15. filled	25. fretted	35. hired
6. halted	16. needed	26. plotted	36. prodded
7. posted	17. claimed	27. stepped	37. risked
8. looked	18. cooked	28. buzzed	38. pelted
9. romped	19. pitched	29. glided	39. lifted
10. mended	20. saved	30. dipped	40. proved

Principle Five in Syllabication

Generally the division of a word into syllables is not changed by the addition of a suffix. EXAMPLES: paint er, fall ing.

☐ 1. Copy the following words, dividing them into syllables.
  2. Mark the vowels.

1. farmer	8. lucky	15. dampen
2. stormy	9. stocking	16. confessing
3. selling	10. broiler	17. puffing
4. burning	11. deaden	18. centralize
5. passable	12. roller	19. golfer
6. refusal	13. tallest	20. shadow
7. service	14. slavish	21. golden

22. spillage	29. claimant	35. cranky
23. vocalize	30. locket	36. pilgrimage
24. childish	31. Lenten	37. foolish
25. selfish	32. feeling	38. hunter
26. basic	33. feverish	39. shrinkage
27. artist	34. formality	40. harpist
28. concordant		

Principle Six in Syllabication

Certain letter combinations that you have had in other exercises are so close that they cannot be separated in dividing words into syllables.

☐ On a separate sheet of paper, show how these words are divided.

1. oi-oy	boiling, employed		7. gh	laughable
2. ou-ow	scouring, coward		8. ph	hyphen
3. au-aw	inaugurate, trawler		9. sh	cashier
4. ei-ie	conceive, believe		10. th	Catholic
5. eu-ew	neutrality, renewal		11. wh	bewhiskered
6. ch-chr	purchase, rechristen		12. ng	singer
			13. qu	inquire

Initial blends (blends that start a syllable):

14. -l implicit
15. -r embrace
16. s- respond
17. t- between

You will find *dw* as the *first* two letters of a word, so there will be no question as to dividing them.

Final blends will give no trouble in dividing into syllables, for they come at the *end,* and if any suffix is added at the end usually this causes no change in syllable division. (See Principle Five in Syllabication, which you have just learned.)

Test on Syllabication

1. Copy the following words, dividing them into syllables.
2. Mark each vowel. (If a letter is silent, make an X through it.)

1. potato
2. holding
3. daffodil
4. obsolete
5. buffalo
6. hydrogen
7. tornado
8. republic
9. tomato
10. performing
11. attendant
12. torpedo
13. juvenile
14. nocturnal

15. rifle
16. planter
17. volcano
18. tricked
19. appendix
20. comprehended
21. blushing
22. tremble
23. decadent
24. music
25. grocer
26. incorporate
27. hummed
28. instantaneous

29. rented
30. tuberculosis
31. innocent.
32. impolite
33. invited
34. mosaic
35. prided
36. glossy
37. enkindle
38. flaxen
39. tormented
40. narcissus

CHAPTER EIGHT

Common First Syllables (Prefixes)

A prefix is a syllable combined with the beginning of a word to modify its meaning. Most prefixes are short and simple; they give little or no difficulty in pronunciation, but a quick recognition of them will enable you to "block out" (using your thumbnail if necessary) this part of a word and consider only what remains. This makes attack on new words much easier.

Knowledge of the meaning of different prefixes, too, will aid you in arriving at the meaning of many new words.

See if you can learn the meanings of all the prefixes on the following pages. Take one or two prefixes at a time. As you learn these prefixes, find other words to . add to the list under each heading.

Pronunciation of *per-* and *pre-*

The prefixes **per-** and **pre-** are frequently confused in reading. **Per-** means "through," and **pre-** means "before" or "in front." The word *prefix* itself means "fixed in front of."

□ Pronunciation of the following words will aid in distinguishing between these two syllables.

1. prepare	15. perceive	29. pre-eminence
2. perform	16. predominate	30. peradventure
3. perplex	17. permeate	31. predilection
4. perfume	18. perspective	32. preponderant
5. premium	19. precipitous	33. performance
6. prevail	20. preconceived	34. perpetration
7. percolate	21. predetermine	35. persecution
8. preventive	22. perjury	36. peremptory
9. premonition	23. pertinent	37. predestination
10. persevere	24. perversity	38. percussion
11. permission	25. preliminary	39. perturbation
12. precise	26. prehistoric	40. prehistoric
13. prescription	27. preconception	
14. preposterous	28. perpendicular	

ab- *from*

1. abnormal	4. abduct	7. absent
2. absorb	5. abstract	8. aberration
3. abrupt	6. abstain	9. abolish

Also with **b** dropped because of
the letter following it:

1. avert

ad- *to*

1. adverb	4. admit	7. adjust
2. advance	5. advocate	8. advantage
3. adhesive	6. adjacent	9. addition

Also with **d** changed because of
letters following it:

1. acquire	4. allude	7. arrest
2. affix	5. annex	8. assist
3. aggressive	6. apply	9. attract

ante- *before*

1. antedate
2. antebellum
3. antecedent
4. anterior
5. antenuptial
6. antechamber
7. antemeridiem (A.M.)
8. antepenult
9. antediluvian

anti- *against*

1. anticlimax
2. antiaircraft
3. antifreeze
4. antitoxin
5. antiseptic
6. antibiotic
7. antibodies
8. antiphony
9. antipathy

circum- *around*

1. circumnavigate
2. circumflex
3. circumspect
4. circumvent
5. circumference
6. circumscribe
7. circumstance
8. circumlocution
9. circumstantiate

Words whose ancestors were related to **circum:**

1. circle
2. circular
3. circulate
4. circuit

con- *with*

1. contract
2. congeal
3. conform
4. congest
5. congregate
6. consolidate
7. concert
8. confide
9. concurrent

Also with **n** changed or dropped:

1. collaborate
2. compress
3. correspond
4. co-operate

de- *down, from*

1. descent
2. deceased
3. debark
4. dehydrate
5. deflate
6. deposit
7. depart
8. degenerate
9. deform

dis- *apart*

1. disappear
2. discard
3. discontent
4. disadvantage
5. disagree
6. dismiss
7. distribute
8. disobey
9. discourage

Also with s changed or dropped:

1. diffuse
2. digress

ex- *out*

1. exit
2. except
3. excel
4. explode
5. external
6. extend
7. export
8. expend
9. expel

Also with x changed or dropped:

1. eccentric
2. effervesce
3. emerge

in- *in*

1. invade
2. invest
3. income
4. inhabit
5. inject
6. infection
7. induct
8. inspect
9. insert

in- *not*

1. incorrect
2. invisible
3. inseparable
4. inappropriate
5. insoluble
6. insufficient
7. ineligible
8. infirm
9. infidel

Also with n changed:

1. illegal
2. immoral
3. irregular

inter- *between, among*

1. interchange
2. international
3. interrupt
4. interview
5. interfere
6. intervene
7. interlude
8. interstate
9. intercede

intra, intro- *within*

1. intramural
2. intramuscular
3. intravenous
4. intracellular
5. intrastate
6. intramolecular
7. introduce
8. introspect
9. introvert

mis- *wrong*

1. mistake
2. mismanage
3. mislead
4. mistreat
5. misbehave
6. misspell
7. misrepresent
8. misdeal
9. misjudge

per- *through*

1. percolate
2. perforate
3. permanent
4. pervade
5. persist
6. perceive
7. perennial
8. permeate
9. perspire

post- *after*

1. postgraduate
2. postscript
3. postmeridiem (P.M.)
4. posthumous
5. postpone
6. posterity
7. postlude
8. posterior
9. postprandial

pre- *before*

1. prepare
2. prescribe
3. precede
4. prelude
5. prefix
6. prevent
7. predict
8. prerequisite
9. preamble

pro- *before, for*

1. proceed
2. protect
3. project
4. protrude
5. propel
6. propose
7. promote
8. prospect
9. produce

re- *again, back*

1. retrace
2. retire
3. revive
4. research
5. return
6. repair
7. report
8. retort
9. release
10. remember

se- *aside*

1. seclude
2. secede
3. secret
4. security
5. sedition
6. separate
7. select
8. secretary
9. secrete

sub- *under, below*

1. submarine
2. subordinate
3. subscribe
4. subdue
5. submerge
6. substitute
7. suburb
8. subversive
9. subside
10. sublet

Also with **b** changed:

1. succumb
2. suffuse
3. suggest
4. support
5. suspect

super- *above*

1. superior
2. superintend
3. supernatural
4. supersede
5. supervise
6. superhuman
7. superficial
8. superfluous
9. superlative

super- may become **sur-** to sound better with
the syllable following:

1. surpass   2. survive

trans- *across, through, beyond*

1. transcription   4. transcend   7. transit
2. transform   5. transfusion   8. translucent
3. transgress   6. transplant   9. transparent

un- *not*

1. unhappy   4. uncover   7. untrue
2. uneven   5. unfaithful   8. unkind
3. uncertain   6. unholy   9. unfortunate

☐ Copy the following words and write *one* after each
word in the first group; *two* after each in the second
group, and *three* after each in the third group. You will
need to use the dictionary to find out what is "enumer-
ated" in the word. Now complete your definition to tell
what is being counted.

uni- *one;* **bi-** *two;* **tri-** *three*

1. uniform   4. university   7. unilateral
2. unicorn   5. unanimous   8. unilingual
3. universe   6. United States

1. bifocals   6. bigamy   11. bivalve
2. bicycle   7. bilateral   12. bicuspid
3. biannual   8. bilingual   13. binocular
4. bicentennial   9. bicameral
5. biceps   10. bipartisan

1. triangle   6. trilateral   11. tricentennial
2. tripod   7. triplet   12. trilogy
3. tricycle   8. triptych   13. trichromatic
4. trident   9. triplicate   14. triennial
5. trifoliate   10. triarchy   15. trinity

Common First Syllables (Prefixes)   99

Test on Prefixes

1. Write the definition of each of the following prefixes. Then write a word that illustrates each prefix.

   a. post
   b. ex
   c. circum

   d. ante
   e. con
   f. sub

   g. trans
   h. super

2. How are the following prefixes alike? Give a word with each.

   a. in
   b. ir
   c. un

3. Write the prefixes meaning *one, two,* and *three.* Write a word with each prefix.

4. Write the definition of each of the following prefixes, and write a word with each prefix.

   a. per
   b. pre
   c. pro

5. What is the difference in meaning between each pair of prefixes below? Write a word with each of the four prefixes.

   a. ante – anti
   b. inter – intra

CHAPTER NINE

Common Last Syllables (Sometimes Suffixes)

Sometimes letters are added at the end of a word instead of at the beginning. You learned that letters added at the beginning change the meaning. There is a difference between saying, "My spelling is correct," and "My spelling is *in*correct." But letters added at the end of a word change meaning hardly at all. They do change the function of the word — the work it does. You may want to say, "I did not spell correctly." Now the letters *-ly* added at the end of the word *correct* make little difference in meaning. But you added *-ly* to make the word do different work — to modify the verb. These letters added at the end of words to change the function are called suffixes.

You saw that the last letter of some prefixes changed to make them "fit" better with certain words. EXAMPLE: *con* (with) became *com* in *compress*. Changes are also made in word endings to make suffixes "fit" better. EXAMPLE: divide — division.

Sometimes a letter combination that looks like a suffix is not truly a suffix. (EXAMPLE: in *badly*, *-ly* is a suffix, but in *lily*, *-ly* is not.) You will find other examples in the lists that follow.

Familiarize yourself thoroughly with the final syllables in the lists. Then, when you encounter a difficult word, see if it has one of these endings. If you find that it has, block it out (with your thumbnail if necessary) and concentrate on what remains of the word. Reading the bracketed information for these words in the dictionary will help greatly in getting their meaning and remembering them.

Later if you hesitate in your reading in pronouncing a word with one of these endings, return to the list with that ending and review the words. Returning to the lists of the more difficult endings from time to time will help you with reading.

-al (-ăl)   usually an adjective ending

1. personal	8. occipital	15. congenial
2. reversal	9. sentimental	16. fraternal
3. radical	10. hypothetical	17. maternal
4. chemical	11. rehearsal	18. puritanical
5. portrayal	12. sensational	19. sartorial
6. editorial	13. centripetal	20. regional
7. baronial	14. centrifugal	

-ate (-āt)   usually a verb ending

1. carbonate	8. emanate	15. saturate
2. duplicate	9. concentrate	16. dominate
3. imitate	10. renovate	17. compensate
4. elevate	11. reciprocate	18. communicate
5. liquidate	12. appropriate	19. reverberate
6. investigate	13. congratulate	20. invigorate
7. evaluate	14. considerate	

-ic (-ĭk)   an adjective ending

1. basic	3. tragic	5. classic
2. heroic	4. civic	6. cubic

7. pelvic
8. metric
9. myopic
10. narcotic
11. nomadic

12. scholastic
13. economic
14. communistic
15. terrific
16. elliptic

17. monastic
18. diabolic
19. enthusiastic
20. realistic

-ful (-fool) *-ful* an adjective ending
-fully (-fool'ĩ) *-ly* an adverb ending

1. wishful
2. wishfully
3. careful
4. carefully
5. awful
6. awfully
7. plentiful

8. plentifully
9. splendidly
10. certainly
11. vehemently
12. pleasantly
13. carelessly
14. purposely

15. rigidly
16. elementally
17. surgically
18. subsequently
19. thoroughly
20. immediately

-ish (-ĭsh) an adjective ending
also a verb ending

1. selfish
2. foolish
3. sluggish
4. childish

5. greenish
6. devilish
7. Spanish
8. peevish

9. feverish
10. outlandish

1. punish
2. furnish
3. accomplish
4. banish

5. cherish
6. famish
7. polish
8. varnish

9. vanish
10. nourish

-ism (-ĭz'm) a noun ending

1. feudalism
2. mysticism
3. egotism
4. realism

5. dogmatism
6. paternalism
7. paganism
8. mesmerism

9. romanticism
10. mechanism
11. ostracism
12. plagiarism

Common Last Syllables (Sometimes Suffixes) 103

13. optimism   16. socialism   19. magnetism
14. pessimism   17. commercialism 20. mannerism
15. spiritualism 18. barbarism

-y (-ĭ)   a noun ending

1. frequency   8. urgency   15. insurgency
2. emergency   9. infancy   16. piracy
3. degeneracy   10. excellency 17. supremacy
4. agency   11. constancy   18. mutiny
5. tendency   12. immediacy   19. drudgery
6. destiny   13. expectancy 20. villainy
7. sorcery   14. hypocrisy

-ity (-ĭ·tĭ)   a noun ending

1. liability   8. probability 15. singularity
2. senility   9. sincerity   16. commodity
3. severity   10. mendacity   17. instrumentality
4. mentality   11. humidity   18. immunity
5. legality   12. electricity 19. curiosity
6. barbarity   13. velocity   20. monstrosity
7. seniority   14. incredulity

-ant (-ănt), -ent (-ĕnt)   common adjective endings
-ance (-ăns), -ence (-ĕns)   noun endings

1. tolerant   8. elegance   15. permanent
2. tolerance   9. convenient   16. permanence
3. evident   10. convenience 17. pertinent
4. evidence   11. dominant   18. pertinence
5. decadent   12. dominance   19. petulant
6. decadence   13. reverent   20. petulance
7. elegant   14. reverence

-ble (-b'l)   an adjective ending
-bly (-blĭ)   an adverb ending

1. stable
2. stably
3. humble
4. humbly
5. notable
6. notably
7. horrible
8. horribly
9. terrible
10. terribly
11. profitable
12. profitably
13. miserable
14. miserably
15. corruptible
16. corruptibly
17. contemptible
18. contemptibly
19. serviceable
20. serviceably

-tive   (-tĭv)
-sive } **(-sĭv)**   adjective endings
-cive }

1. positive
2. narrative
3. automotive
4. decisive
5. cohesive
6. persuasive
7. conducive
8. retentive
9. sensitive
10. explosive
11. preparative
12. degenerative
13. successive
14. alternative
15. digestive
16. inventive
17. communicative
18. comparative
19. constructive
20. instinctive

-tion (-shŭn)
-sion (shŭn or   noun endings
      -zhŭn)

1. addition
2. convention
3. nomination
4. corruption
5. formation
6. admiration
7. imposition
8. situation
9. temptation
10. consideration
11. evaporation
12. speculation
13. prescription
14. participation
15. sensation
16. indignation
17. proclamation
18. accommodation
19. fumigation
20. stimulation

21. meditation
22. superstition
23. toleration
24. radiation
25. importation
26. duplication
27. consecration
28. conjugation
29. dilation
30. subordination
31. distinction
32. recession
33. excursion
34. precision
35. extension
36. diversion
37. confusion
38. admission
39. provision
40. emulsion

41. adhesion
42. propulsion
43. session
44. division
45. television
46. version
47. submission
48. confession
49. permission
50. decision
51. convulsion
52. incision
53. reversion
54. succession
55. compulsion
56. submersion
57. dissension
58. secession
59. profession
60. comprehension

-ous (-ŭs)   an adjective ending

1. enormous
2. porous
3. famous
4. populous
5. momentous
6. ominous
7. delirious

8. conspicuous
9. contagious
10. multitudinous
11. vicarious
12. obsequious
13. carnivorous
14. herbivorous

15. supercilious
16. marvelous
17. venomous
18. obstreperous
19. disastrous
20. innocuous

Notice that words ending in **-ous** are all *adjectives*. *Nouns* that end in **-us**: *hippopotamus, hibiscus, terminus, crocus, radius,* are unrelated to the kind of words listed above.

-tious
-cious (**-shŭs**) adjective endings

1. delicious
2. fallacious
3. contentious
4. loquacious
5. capricious
6. ostentatious
7. spacious
8. precocious
9. fractious
10. conscious
11. voracious
12. licentious
13. pernicious
14. mendacious
15. specious
16. pretentious
17. pugnacious
18. avaricious
19. facetious
20. officious

-tial
-sial (**-shăl**) adjective endings
-cial

1. partial
2. martial
3. facial
4. palatial
5. nuptial
6. racial
7. glacial
8. essential
9. penitential
10. commercial
11. beneficial
12. torrential
13. special
14. credential
15. sequential
16. pestilential
17. substantial
18. controversial
19. confidential
20. circumstantial

Test on Final Syllables

Tell the final syllable of each word and what it indicates.

1. friction
2. precious
3. accession
4. creditable
5. creditably
6. permanent
7. permanence
8. courtesy
9. legalism
10. symbolic
11. cautious
12. salvation
13. sacrificial
14. idyllic
15. predominant
16. predominance
17. vertical
18. incorporate
19. tangible
20. tangibly

21. crucial
22. surreptitious
23. initiation
24. scornful
25. scornfully
26. designate
27. algebraic
28. ostracism
29. plausible
30. plausibly
31. snobbish
32. personality
33. perspective
34. commercialize
35. legislation
36. erosive
37. demoralize
38. garrulous
39. regeneracy
40. formality
41. conservative
42. perspiration
43. celebrity
44. readable
45. rigorous
46. eccentricity
47. symphonic
48. incongruous
49. Oriental
50. excavation
51. luscious
52. precipitate
53. different
54. difference
55. considerable
56. considerably

57. paganism
58. phonetic
59. culminate
60. judicial
61. sympathize
62. transmission
63. ambitious
64. commentary
65. tremendous
66. explorative
67. transgression
68. sagacious
69. crystallize
70. recuperative
71. capacious
72. percussion
73. pestiferous
74. illusion
75. legislative
76. spontaneity
77. corruptible
78. official
79. embryonic
80. astigmatism
81. expatriation
82. vicious
83. permissible
84. liberality
85. constancy
86. conversion
87. pertinacious
88. reducible
89. potential
90. lymphatic
91. explosion
92. reversible

93. combination
94. resilient
95. resilience
96. clannish
97. pathetic
98. coagulate
99. establish
100. cosmic
101. culpable
102. neutrality
103. contiguous
104. sociable
105. controversion
106. remarkable

107. remarkably
108. gregarious
109. revision
110. raucous
111. audition
112. dynamic
113. migration
114. physical .
115. persuasion
116. availability
117. suspension
118. experimental
119. equinoctial
120. differential

CHAPTER TEN

Common Word Roots

A well-known magazine in a study of 20,000 common English words found that over 12,000 were based on Greek or Latin.

So many English words come from *one* Greek or Latin root that if you learn *one* root, you have a key to an entire family of words. EXAMPLE: from *spir,* a Latin root meaning "breathe," we have the following list:

expire	aspire	respire
inspire	conspire	suspire
perspire	transpire	spirit

There are several other forms for some of the words above: *perspiration, aspiration,* etc.

Two Greek roots, *pachy* and *derm,* meaning "thick" and "skin," respectively, are combined into one word in our language, *pachyderm.* When the circus comes to town and your newspaper says that the pachyderms led the parade, do you know what animals are meant?

In the following exercises you will have some common word roots. Knowledge of these roots and of how words are made will make you more word-conscious, and will result in your becoming a better speaker and a better reader.

tele *far* (Greek)

□ Make a word by using **tele** as a prefix for each part of a word that is given and defined below.

1. gram (write)   3. phone (sound)   5. scope (watcher)
2. graph (write)   4. photo (light)   6. vision (seeing)

dent *tooth* (Latin)

□ Choose a word from this list to complete each sentence.

1. dentist   3. dentifrice   5. indention
2. denture   4. dental   6. indentured

1. An improperly fitted _____ can cause much discomfort.
2. Toothpaste is one form of _____ .
3. The use of _____ floss stimulates the gums.
4. One should visit a _____ twice each year.
5. Paragraph _____s have the appearance of irregular teeth.
6. An _____ servant held one part of a written contract edged with teethlike notches that matched the other part held by the servant's owner.

chron *time* (Greek)

□ Choose a word from this list to complete each sentence.

1. chronicle   3. chronic   5. chronometer
2. synchronize 4. chronologically 6. anachronism

1. The poor fellow has had a sinus infection so long that it seems his trouble has become _____ .
2. Would you call a lady's hoop skirt for street wear an _____ ?

3. A _____ is an instrument that keeps time with great accuracy.
4. Much of the literature of the Colonial period of America consists of sermons and _____s.
5. The early movie makers could not _____ voice and action.
6. One test question in history was to list the wars of our country _____.

aud *hear* (Latin)

☐ Choose a word from this list to complete each sentence.

1. audience   3. auditorium   5. audible
2. auditory   4. audition   6. auditor

1. One who takes a college course not for credit but merely to hear the lectures is called an _____.
2. The _____ nerve connects the ear and the brain.
3. Elena hopes to secure a position with the orchestra. She will be given an _____ Monday afternoon.
4. The ticking of the clock is barcly _____.
5. There was a large and enthusiastic _____ at the concert last evening.
6. We heard a fine address in the _____ today.

mort *death* (Latin)

☐ Choose a word from this list to complete each sentence.

1. morgue   4. immortal   7. post-mortem
2. mortgage   5. mortification
3. mortal   6. mortician

1. A _____ is a professional undertaker.
2. The human soul is _____.

3. All of the animal world is _____.
4. Bodies of those found dead are taken to a _____ for identification.
5. A *gage* is a pledge. A _____ originally meant that a *pledge* was made on an owner's property, and that the owner's rights to the profits from that property became *dead*.
6. _____ is a "dying" of the flesh or of the self-respect.
7. A _____ is an examination after death.

rupt   *break* (Latin)

☐ Choose a word from this list to complete each sentence.

1. erupt	3. corrupt	5. interrupt
2. abrupt	4. disrupt	6. rupture

1. In what year did Vesuvius _____ and destroy Pompeii?
2. The fire drill will _____ all classes at ten o'clock.
3. Adela felt insulted and made an _____ departure.
4. The _____ of friendly relations between the two countries is a serious matter.
5. The question of return of prisoners of war will _____ negotiations.
6. Association with the unrighteous will _____ the weak.

☐ What other forms can you give for each word listed above?

tort   *twist* (Latin)

☐ Choose a word from the following list to complete each sentence.

1. extort	4. contortion	7. tortuous
2. retort	5. tortoise
3. distort	6. torture

1. The _____ gets its name from the fact that it has twisted feet.
2. Religious freedom ended _____ of those whose beliefs were not recognized.
3. Factory owners do not _____ great labor for little pay as in earlier days.
4. The children were amused at the clown's facial _____s.
5. The mountain road was a _____ trail.
6. The police officer did not seem suprised at the motorist's _____.
7. The newspaper did not _____ the words of the secretary's report.

$$\left.\begin{array}{l}\textbf{pel}\\\textbf{puls}\end{array}\right\}\ \textit{drive}\ (\text{Latin})$$

☐ Choose a word from the first column of this list to complete each sentence.

1. expel	7. expulsion
2. propel	8. propulsion
3. compel	9. compulsion
4. dispel
5. repel	10. repulsion
6. impel	11. impulsion

1. Happenings of the day _____led all hopes of our leaving early the next morning.
2. The similar poles of the magnets _____led each other.
3. The student was _____led from the university for cheating on an exam.

4. I felt _____led to defend the rights of pedestrians.
5. The driver _____led the disorderly man to leave the bus.
6. The boat was _____led by an outboard motor.

☐ Why is the final consonant doubled before the ending *-ed?*

☐ Make up sentences using the noun forms numbered 7 through 11. What other forms are there for 10 and 11?

fid *faith* (Latin)

☐ Choose a word from this list to complete each sentence.

1. confident   4. fidelity   7. Semper Fidelis
2. fiduciary   5. infidel
3. Fido   6. confidential

1. Dogs are such faithful animals that many are frequently named _____.
2. Are you _____ that it will happen?
3. If information is not to be repeated, it is _____ information.
4. Patriots are noted for their _____ to their country.
5. The motto of the Marine Corps is _____.
6. One who does not follow the accepted religion is called an _____.
7. The relationships between depositors and their bank are _____.

cred
creed } *belief* (Latin)

☐ Choose a word from the following list to complete each sentence.

1. creed
2. credentials
3. credible
4. incredulous
5. credit
6. credence
7. credulity

1. The department store grants _____ to all employees of the factory.
2. Do you give more _____ to the story of the hunter or to that of the guide?
3. There was an _____ look on the teacher's face as Miguel gave his excuse.
4. Do you know the _____ of your church?
5. You should submit your _____ when applying for a job in that store.
6. The story of "Little Red Riding Hood" seems _____ to a small child.
7. The motorist detected some sign of _____ in the face of the officer, and elaborated the explanation.

cide   *kill* (Latin)

☐ Using your dictionary, tell who or what was killed in each case.

1. suicide
2. homicide
3. fratricide
4. patricide
5. sororicide
6. matricide
7. uxoricide
8. genocide
9. infanticide
10. fungicide
11. germicide
12. insecticide
13. pesticide
14. regicide
15. parricide

clud } *shut* (Latin)
clus

☐ Choose one of these six words to complete each sentence.

1. exclude
2. include
3. conclude
4. preclude
5. occlude
6. seclude

1. Lucy forgot to glue the pieces together because the directions did not _____ this step.
2. No doubt Mary, Eleanor, Jane, and Louise will _____ that they should not stay longer.
3. Oculists _____ one eye while testing the other one.
4. The coach did not permit Leonard to play, because he had to _____ everyone over eighteen years of age.
5. John Henry's participation in professional tennis will _____ his playing in the spring amateur tournament.
6. Margaret will have to _____ herself until her theme is written.

□ Make up sentences of your own, using the noun forms numbered 7 through 12.

7. exclusion
8. inclusion
9. conclusion
10. preclusion
11. occlusion
12. seclusion

gress *step* (Latin)

□ Choose a word from this list to complete each sentence.

1. progress
2. digress
3. Congress
4. egress
5. transgress
6. ingress
7. aggression
8. regression
9. retrogression

1. The _____ of the United States is in session.
2. War was caused by _____ of the dictator state.
3. To _____ that law meant death.
4. To _____ often spoils your story.
5. Do not be discouraged if you _____ slowly at first.
6. Provide other means of _____ in case of fire.
7. We hoped for progress, but instead there was _____.

118   **WORD ATTACK**

8. Every place of ＿＿＿ was crowded at the stadium because everyone wanted to see the game.
9. Destruction of their libraries will cause ＿＿＿ in their culture.
10. There is a certain amount of ＿＿＿ in everyone, but most people are able to channel this drive in worthwhile ways.

flu *flow* (Latin)

☐ Choose a word from this list to complete each sentence.

1. fluctuate	5. confluence	9. affluent
2. influx	6. influence	10. flux
3. fluently	7. reflux	
4. superfluous	8. influenza	

1. The professor speaks three languages ＿＿＿.
2. The minister of the little church had great ＿＿＿ in the community.
3. An epidemic of ＿＿＿ in ancient days was attributed to the influence of the heavenly bodies.
4. The stock market ＿＿＿s from day to day.
5. At harvest time in the Middle West there is a great ＿＿＿ of laborers.
6. The moon governs the ＿＿＿ and the ＿＿＿ of the tides.
7. Prospectors in California in 1849 found gold and returned very ＿＿＿.
8. It has been proposed that our ＿＿＿ wheat be sold to other countries.
9. At the ＿＿＿ of the two rivers is a beautiful waterfall.
10. Although the attorney's plea was very moving, it did not ＿＿＿ the jury's decision.

ced
ceed } *go, move* (Latin)
cess

☐ Choose a word from this list to complete each sentence.

1. exceed   4. proceed   7. secede
2. accede   5. precede   8. concede
3. succeed   6. intercede   9. recede

1. After these arrangements, we hope to _____ with our plans for the trip.
2. The two players quarreled until the coach had to _____.
3. Waters of the lake did not _____ for three weeks.
4. We were fearful that expenses would _____ our available funds.
5. The president will _____ all others in the procession.
6. Eugene Hsi will _____ Ann Blair as class president.
7. Which was the first state to _____ from the Union?
8. Mother would not _____ to our wishes until we promised to return early.
9. I am sure that Eleanor will _____ that you were right when you explain.

☐ Make a noun by using **-cess** or **-cession** instead of **-cede** or **-ceed** for each word listed above, except for the fifth. How must the fifth be changed to make a noun?

graph
graphy } *write* (Greek)

☐ Write the numbers 1 through 10 on your paper. Beside each number write a word, using **graph** or **graphy** as the ending to the part given. Following the completed word, give a definition. You may use the dictionary.

1. photo (light)
2. phono (sound)
3. steno (small)
4. geo (earth)
5. biblio (book)
6. auto (self)
7. bio (life)
8. carto (map)
9. para (aside from)
10. calli (beautiful)

11. What use do you make of *graphite?*
12. A _____ic description of a scene is like a picture drawn of the scene.

tract   *draw* (Latin)

☐ Choose a word from this list to complete each sentence.

1. attract
2. subtract
3. retract
4. extract
5. abstract
6. traction
7. detract
8. contract
9. distract
10. protractor

1. What remains when you _____ 24 from 48?
2. Do you think the red shutters _____ from the appearance of the house?
3. Did you make a satisfactory _____ with the carpenter for the job?
4. The newspaper was asked to _____ its statement that the referee favored the home team.
5. Do you find that radio music _____ you when you are studying?
6. Broken legs and arms are frequently put in _____ while healing.
7. The restaurant lowered its prices this summer to _____ more tourists.
8. Manufacturers of perfumes _____ fragrances from flowers.
9. A lawyer often writes an _____ of a legal case.
10. An engineer, designer, or toolmaker uses a _____.

$$\left.\begin{array}{l}\textbf{man} \\ \textbf{manu}\end{array}\right\} \textit{hand} \text{ (Latin)}$$

☐ Choose a word from this list to complete each sentence.

1. manicure	5. manipulate	9. manner
2. manual	6. emancipate	10. manage
3. manufacture	7. manacle	
4. manuscript	8. amanuensis	

1. Picking cotton is _____ labor.
2. The original _____ of a poem by Sappho was recently found.
3. The criminal was _____d to two guards.
4. Did you have a _____ this afternoon?
5. Products were originally made by hand. We still say things are _____d, even though we use machines.
6. Slaves were _____d after the War Between the States.
7. The daughter of the blind poet John Milton was his _____.
8. One supervisor can _____ a crew of workers.
9. Can you _____ the canoe so as to avoid the current?
10. The way people act is their _____, or "what they do with their hands."

phil *love* (Greek)

☐ Choose a word from this list to complete each sentence.

1. philatelist	5. Philadelphia	9. philology
2. philanderer	6. philanthropist	10. Anglophile
3. Philip	7. philosophy	
4. bibliophile	8. Philharmonic	

1. Phoebe Hearst gave much of her fortune for the establishing of libraries, schools, and hospitals. She was a great _____.
2. Louise Dale Boyd has an unusual collection of stamps. She is an enthusiastic _____.
3. The Philadelphia _____ Society has done much to promote young composers.
4. Henry grew to love the people of England while he was a student there. He might be called an _____.
5. The common Christian name _____ means a lover of horses.
6. The girls are accusing the young man of being quite a _____.
7. Eleanor Roosevelt who had a large private library, was a noted _____.
8. _____ means the love of wisdom.
9. Anita served as translator of several languages at the conference. She has made a study of _____.
10. _____ is the "city of brotherly love."

pan *all* (Greek)

☐ Choose a word from this list to complete each sentence.

1. pancreas
2. panacea
3. pandemonium
4. pantomime
5. Pandora
6. Pantheon
7. panchromatic
8. panorama
9. Pan American Airways
10. Pan American Games

1. The _____ is an organ of the body that is "all flesh."
2. All countries of America compete in the _____.
3. _____ means "all mimic."
4. A _____ affords a wide view of the scene.
5. A _____ film reproduces all colors.

Common Word Roots   123

6. One can fly over all of North and South America on _____.
7. There is no _____ for all ills.
8. The _____ was built to honor all the Roman gods.
9. _____ was given all the gifts that the gods could bestow.
10. When you hear a racket that sounds like all the demons, you call it a _____.

$$\left.\begin{matrix} \textbf{junct} \\ \textbf{jug} \end{matrix}\right\}$$ *join or yoke* (Latin)

☐ Choose a word from this list to complete each sentence.

1. junction   4. conjugal   7. injunction
2. conjugate   5. conjunction   8. subjugate
3. juncture   6. adjunct

1. The word *and* is a _____.
2. The coach was derailed at the _____ of the two railroads.
3. The retired couple lived in _____ bliss for many years.
4. A light meter is a useful _____ to camera equipment.
5. We had lost our tickets and had no more money. At this _____ we did not know what to do.
6. The judge issued an _____ preventing the company from taking possession of the building.
7. The officers with difficulty _____ed the thief.
8. What do you do when you _____ a verb?

sect   *cut* (Latin)

☐ Choose a word from this list to complete each sentence.

1. bisect	4. dissect	7. sect
2. intersect	5. insect	8. sector
3. vivisection	6. section	9. sectarian

1. In biology class today we will _____ a frog.
2. Members of this little church are a _____ of the Baptist Church.
3. Why is a wasp a good example of an _____?
4. Liberty Street _____ s Branch Avenue three blocks from here.
5. The main _____ of his ranch is across the state boundary line.
6. The diameter of a circle _____ s the circle.
7. The radii divided the circle into ten _____ s.
8. Experimental surgery performed on living animals is called _____.
9. Some _____ s oppose a community church.

ora   *speech, prayer* (Latin)

☐ Choose a word from this list to complete each sentence.

1. oral	5. oration	9. inexorable
2. oratorical	6. orator	10. orate
3. oracle	7. oratorio	
4. oracular	8. oratory	

1. George won a prize for _____.
2. People who want to speak out for their cause are allowed to _____ in the park.
3. Senator Williams delivered a long _____ at the Fourth of July exercises.
4. Three _____ s will speak at the meeting of the veterans.
5. Do you prefer _____ or written examinations?

6. The Greeks were influenced by what the _____ at Delphi said.
7. We want to hear the _____ at the church on Easter Sunday.
8. Our school was victor in the _____ contest last night.
9. The old chief spoke in _____ tones about the coming spring rains.
10. Julie begged to use the car, but her parents were _____.

cept *take* (Latin)

☐ Choose a word from this list to answer each of the following questions.

1. accept	5. intercept	8. perceptible
2. except	6. receptacle	9. deception
3. concept	7. receptive	10. inception
4. precept		

1. Which word means capable of being taken in through the senses?
2. Which word means to take in?
3. Which word means to take out or to leave out?
4. Which word means inclined toward taking in?
5. Which word means to take between its start and finish?
6. Which word means something that takes in?
7. Which word means something that has taken form in the mind?
8. Which word means a taking or leading away from the truth?
9. Which word means a beginning?
10. Which word means a teaching or example?

☐ What different forms can you list for each of the ten words?

$$\left.\begin{array}{l} \textbf{script} \\ \textbf{scrib} \end{array}\right\} \textit{write} \text{ (Latin)}$$

☐ Choose a word from this list to fit each meaning.

1. describe
2. postscript
3. transcribe
4. proscribe
5. prescribe
6. conscription
7. scribble
8. inscription
9. superscription
10. subscribe
11. ascribe
12. manuscript

1. Something written at the end of a letter?
2. Something written on the outside of an envelope?
3. Something "written" on a tombstone?
4. To write in shorthand and then on a typewriter?
5. To "write" a remedy for a person who is ill?
6. To "write" about the appearance of something?
7. To write carelessly?
8. To "write" a prohibition against doing something?
9. To "write" your name in agreement to purchase a magazine?
10. A "writing" of names for compulsory armed service?
11. The _____ of the play has been _____d either to Shakespeare or to Bacon.

$$\left.\begin{array}{l} \textbf{pote} \\ \textbf{poss} \end{array}\right\} \textit{power} \text{ (Latin)}$$

☐ Choose a word from this list to complete each sentence.

1. impotent
2. potential
3. potency
4. potentate
5. potent
6. posse
7. plenipotentiary (*pleni-* full)
8. potentiality
9. omnipotent (*omni-* all)
10. possible

1. Soft drinks are not _____.
2. Repeated veto by a few made the council _____.

3. This ambassador was our _____ in the Middle East.
4. Every gun is a _____ murder weapon.
5. The patient did not realize the _____ of the pills.
6. No one can estimate the _____ of satellites for future education.
7. A large _____ is now on the trail of the escaped prisoner.
8. Several countries are still ruled by a _____.
9. Only God is _____.
10. It is not _____ to run fast in this deep snow.

dict   *tell, say* (Latin)

☐ Choose a word from this list to answer each of the following questions.

1. dictionary   5. contradict   9. edict
2. dictate   6. predict   10. verdict
3. interdict   7. dictator
4. diction   8. Dictaphone

1. Which means to *tell* about the future?
2. Which is a person who *tells* others what to do or not to do?
3. Which *tells* the meaning of words?
4. Which means the choice of words in which we *tell* our thoughts?
5. Which means to *say* that something is wrong?
6. Which is a device into which something is *told?*
7. Which means to *tell* so that another may write the words down?
8. Which is a public notice proclaiming a command, law, or rule of conduct?
9. Which may be a decree forbidding persons to receive the sacraments?
10. Which is the name for a decision *told* by a jury?

$$\left.\begin{array}{l} \textbf{viv} \\ \textbf{vit} \end{array}\right\} \textit{live} \text{ (Latin)}$$

☐ Choose a word from this list to complete each sentence.

1. vivid	5. viable	9. vitality
2. revive	6. vivacious	10. viand
3. survive	7. conviviality	
4. vivisection	8. devitalize	

1. A rescue squad was unable to _____ the child.
2. The dancer's spirit and _____ excited the audience.
3. Some people have opposed _____ because of their love of animals.
4. Everyone enjoyed the _____ of a merry group of passengers.
5. You could well imagine her a model, for she is such a _____ girl.
6. Jane should be an author because she has a very _____ imagination.
7. Thousands will be unable to _____ the famine caused by the floods.
8. The table was covered with _____s of all kinds.
9. The seeds we planted evidently were not _____.
10. The seeds had been _____d by years of storage.

ped *foot* (Latin)

☐ Choose the word from this list that answers each question.

1. pedal	5. biped	9. impediment
2. peddle	6. centipede	10. expedite
3. pedestal	7. peddler	
4. pedestrian	8. impede	

1. What has two feet?
2. Which travels on foot?
3. Which is a lever for foot action?
4. Which has a hundred (or many) feet?
5. Which is a base of a column or statue?
6. Which means to carry wares about on foot?
7. Which is a stumbling block (foot tangler)?
8. Which means to put the foot out (to rush)?
9. Who sells from door to door (on foot mainly)?
10. Which means to hold back (obstruct the foot)?

leg *law* (Latin)

□ Choose a word from this list to complete each sentence.

1. legal	5. legislature	9. legalize
2. illegal	6. legality	10. legacy
3. legitimate	7. legislator	
4. legation	8. legatee	

1. It is _____ to park double on this narrow street.
2. Smaller countries are represented abroad by _____s, instead of embassies.
3. Henry's _____ from his grandmother was not withheld by the court.
4. Ira's sister is an Ohio _____.
5. In some states lotteries are recognized by law and are _____.
6. Miriam is the chief _____ in her uncle's will.
7. The action taken by the company was not _____, and it had to pay a fine.
8. _____s make the laws of the land.
9. A new law will _____ a sales tax.
10. The courts are testing the _____ of the will.

☐ From another Latin word meaning "to read" we have borrowed the same root, **leg,** with another meaning. What does *legible* mean? *Illegible? Legibility?*

$$\left.\begin{array}{l} \textbf{voc} \\ \textbf{vok} \end{array}\right\} \quad voice, \ call \ \text{(Latin)}$$

☐ Choose a word or words from this list to complete each sentence.

1. vocal	6. advocate	11. invocation
2. revoke	7. vocation	12. vocalize
3. provoke	8. vocalist	13. avocation
4. revocable	9. vociferous	14. vocabulary
5. irrevocable	10. convocation	

1. Words once uttered are never wholly _____. They are to some extent _____.
2. Church services usually begin with an _____, or a calling for divine blessing or aid.
3. To live a full life, one should have both a _____ and an _____.
4. Both churches and schools _____ better facilities for recreation for young people.
5. The boys and girls were quite _____ in their demands that the orchestra give an encore.
6. The mayor would not _____ the order limiting vacations to two weeks.
7. The total number of words you know makes up your _____.
8. After dinner we enjoyed both instrumental and _____ numbers.
9. Many members of former graduating classes attend the _____ every year.

10. It is a bad habit to _____ when you are doing "silent" reading.
11. Whether she sang opera or spirituals, Marian Anderson received world-wide acclaim as a truly great _____.
12. A massive letter campaign _____d the council to take action.

$$\left.\begin{array}{l} \textbf{duct} \\ \textbf{duc} \end{array}\right\} \textit{lead} \text{ (Latin)}$$

☐ Choose a word from this list to answer each of the following questions.

1. conduct	5. produce	9. abduct
2. aqueduct	6. introduce	10. deduct
3. induce	7. viaduct	
4. induct	8. reduce	

1. Which means to lead on or to persuade another?
2. Which means to lead among others and make acquainted?
3. Which means to lead with or to guide?
4. Which means to lead into?
5. Which carries water over a gorge or river?
6. Which is a bridgelike structure carrying roads over valleys and rivers?
7. Which means to lead backward?
8. Which means to make, or to lead forward into existence?
9. Which means to lead away from or to subtract?
10. Which means to kidnap?

☐ What other words can you add to those listed?

pend ⎫
pens ⎭ *hang* (Latin)

☐ Choose a word from this list to complete each sentence below.

1. expend
2. pendulum
3. suspense
4. depend

5. impending
6. pending
7. pendant
8. suspension

9. suspend
10. append

1. To and fro swung the _____ of the old clock.
2. My sister received a _____ for a birthday present.
3. The treasurer presented an estimate of how much the club would receive and _____ .
4. Your order is being held _____ receipt of information as to the sizes you wish.
5. How far we drive today will _____ on the weather.
6. The family were in terrible _____ until they heard from John.
7. We crossed the beautiful _____ bridge over the Hudson River.
8. _____ further action on my order until frost begins.
9. They walked cautiously, as if aware of the _____ disaster.
10. I want to _____ a postscript to that letter.

port *carry* (Latin)

☐ Choose a word from this list to answer each question.

1. export
2. import
3. portable
4. port
5. portfolio

6. report
7. comport
8. disport
9. support
10. deport

11. deportment
12. porter
13. portage
14. transport

1. Which carries baggage?
2. Which means to carry into a country?
3. Which means to carry out of a country?
4. Which describes articles which can be carried by hand?
5. Which does a country do to rid itself of someone undesirable?
6. Which is the carrying of boats overland between bodies of water.
7. Which is a place where ships come, carrying goods to and from foreign countries?
8. Which is a case for carrying loose papers?
9. Which do you carry back with you?
10. Which do we give our candidates and causes?
11. Which means to play (to carry ourselves away from work)?
12. Which means the manner in which we "carry" ourselves in society?
13. Which means to carry across boundaries, oceans, etc.?
14. Which means to conduct oneself?

ject   *throw* (Latin)

☐ Choose a word from this list to complete each sentence.

1. object	6. subject	11. reject
2. inject	7. interject	12. rejection
3. project	8. adjective	13. dejection
4. projectile	9. eject	14. conjecture
5. projection	10. injection	

1. Operators of public gathering places sometimes are forced to _____ disorderly characters.
2. The nose is a _____ on the face.

3. A rifle fires a _____ at its target.
4. The students were depressed after the _____ of their plan.
5. This young man's _____ did not last long.
6. Do not _____ such remarks in serious conversation.
7. The young poet thought the publisher would _____ her poem.
8. We thought the judge should not _____ the prisoner to further punishment.
9. My influenza was cured by an _____ of penicillin.
10. The work was so heavy that I did not want to undertake the _____.
11. A word added to a noun or pronoun as a modifier is an _____.
12. We made all plans for the trip, not knowing that Father would _____.
13. All evidence considered, my _____ was that the Fongs wanted to leave early.
14. Between yours and Pat's dissertations, may I _____ a few remarks?

$$\left.\begin{array}{l} \textbf{mit} \\ \textbf{mis} \end{array}\right\}$$ *send or let go* (Latin)

□ Choose a word from this list to complete each sentence.

1. admit	6. dismiss	11. committee
2. omit	7. manumit	12. commissary
3. commit	8. submit	13. mission
4. permit	9. missionary	14. emit
5. remit	10. intermission	

1. Our principal will _____ all classes at noon when the parade passes.
2. We were afraid we would _____ some name when we made our list.

3. Between the second and third acts of the play we will have a long _____.
4. Do you prefer that we _____ the money by bank check or post-office money order?
5. Jane's grandmother was a _____ to India.
6 The judge decided to _____ the thief to jail for thirty days.
7. Ten were appointed to the _____ to investigate cafeteria prices.
8. The committee will _____ to the movie everyone who brings a pound of food.
9. My parents _____ me to have the car on Friday nights.
10. All kinds of food, clothing, tools, and house furnishings may be bought at the new _____.
11. I intend to _____ my proposition.
12. Bakeshops _____ tantalizing odors.
13. In some countries people buy caged birds to _____ them in hopes of receiving a blessing therefor.
14. To sell tickets was my particular _____ in calling on alumni.

□ Give other forms for some of the words listed above.

$$\left.\begin{array}{l}\textbf{spec} \\ \textbf{spic} \\ \textbf{spect}\end{array}\right\}\ \textit{look}\ \text{(Latin)}$$

□ Choose a word from this list to answer each question.

1. aspect	7. speculate	13. spectrum
2. inspect	8. circumspect	14. specter
3. respect	9. retrospect	15. expect
4. spectacles	10. conspicuous	16. suspect
5. prospect	11. spectacle	17. introspect
6. spectator	12. specimen	

1. Which one is a looker-on?
2. Which is a display magnificent to look upon?
3. Which means to look back upon with appreciation?
4. Which looks ghostly?
5. Which may be looked upon as a sample of its kind?
6. Which is a device that aids in looking?
7. Which means to look forward to?
8. Which means to look into in order to evaluate?
9. Which is a series of colors we look upon when light is refracted?
10. Which may be looked upon as the likely future?
11. Which means to look to future profit in a changing market?
12. Which means to look upon as guilty on slight proof?
13. Which means looking around and being cautious?
14. Which means to look into and examine one's own mind?
15. Which means causing many to look?
16. Which means the "look" or appearance of something?
17. Which means to look back over the past?

$$\left.\begin{matrix} \textbf{vert} \\ \textbf{vers} \end{matrix}\right\} \quad turn \text{ (Latin)}$$

☐ Choose a word from this list to answer each question.

1. avert	8. convert	15. adversity
2. advertise	9. vertebra	16. divert
3. versus	10. adversary	17. subversive
4. reverse	11. introvert	18. vertigo
5. diversion	12. extrovert	19. transverse
6. versatile	13. revert	
7. invert	14. version	

1. Which describes a person who turns from one skill to another with ease?
2. Which is a series of small bones turning easily?
3. Which means to turn back to something said or done before?
4. Which is to turn upside down?
5. Which is a dizziness (a turning) in the head?
6. Which is a person who likes to be alone?
7. Which is a person who does not like being alone?
8. Which means to cause people to turn their attention to?
9. Which may indicate the opposite of something?
10. Which is to turn someone with you in your opinion?
11. Which is a turning from labors?
12. Which describes efforts of undercover workers to turn a government into another form?
13. Which is a person turned against you?
14. Which is an unfortunate happening?
15. Which means to turn out of the way of or avoid?
16. Which means to turn someone's attention away from something?
17. Which means a story from one point of view?
18. Which means turned against, as in a football game?
19. Which means turned across?

Test One on Word Roots

Number 1 through 40 on your paper. For each word in this list, write only the part of it that means the same as the word beside it. You will be picking out the word roots, and only the roots will appear on your paper.

1. intermission — send
2. irrevocable — voice
3. aqueduct — lead
4. intercept — take
5. auditorium — hear
6. mortification — death

7. homicide – kill
8. contradict – say
9. potentiality – power
10. conclude – shut
11. tortuous – twist
12. bibliography – write
13. produce – lead
14. impediment – foot
15. conviviality – live
16. suspension – hand
17. interruption – break
18. superfluous – flow
19. pantheon – all
20. conspicuous – see
21. incredible – belief
22. legality – law
23. permit – send
24. chronological – time
25. retract – draw
26. manuscript – hand
27. compulsion – drive
28. diversion – turn
29. confidential – faith
30. portfolio – carry
31. recede – go
32. amanuensis – hand
33. telephoto – far
34. conjecture – throw
35. transgress – step
36. philanderer – love
37. indention – tooth
38. sectional – cut
39. oratory – speech
40. adjunct – join

Test Two on Word Roots

Copy the list of roots from the Table of Contents. After each root write its definition and some word containing that root.

B 8
C 9
D 0
E 1
F 2
G 3
H 4
I 5
J 6